THE
INFINITE
MIRROR

Other books by Master Sheng-yen:

Getting the Buddha Mind
Poetry of Enlightenment – Poems by Ancient Ch'an Masters
Faith in Mind
Ox Herding at Morgan's Bay

THE INFINITE MIRROR

Ts'ao-Tung Ch'an:
Commentaries on
Inquiry Into Matching Halves
and
Song of the Precious Mirror Samadhi

Master Sheng-yen

Editor	Christopher Marano
Editorial Assistance	Harry Miller
	Stuart Lachs
	Jonathan Bardin
	Nancy Makso
Translators	Ming Yee Wang
	Pei-gwang Dowiat
Transcribers	Dorothy Weiner
	Nancy Makso
Book Design	Page Simon
Cover Design	Page Simon
	Trish Ing
Production	Trish Ing

Dharma Drum Publications is the publishing activity of

Institute of Chung-Hwa Buddhist Culture
90-56 Corona Avenue
Elmhurst, New York 11373

Library of Congress Catalog Card Number 90-81014
ISBN 0-9609854-4-1

Table of Contents

Preface

Inquiry Into Matching Halves, written by Shih-t'ou Hsi-ch'ien, and Song of the Precious Mirror Samadhi, written by Tung-shan Liang-chieh, are considered the two most important works of the Ts'ao-tung (Soto) Sect of Ch'an Buddhism. The Ts'ao-tung sect's origin can be traced directly to Shih-t'ou Hsi-ch'ien (700-790), and indirectly to his grandmaster, Sixth Patriarch Hui-neng (638-713). However, the Ts'ao-tung sect derives its name from its two most famous patriarchs, Ch'an masters Tung-shan Liang-chieh (807-869) and Ts'ao-shan Pen-chi (840-901).

Shih-t'ou had many disciples, among them Ch'an masters Yao-shan Wei-yen (745-828) and T'ien-huang Tao-wu (754-807). Like Shih-t'ou, Yao-shan Wei-yen transmitted the Dharma to many descendants, including two important Ch'an masters, Yün-yen T'an-sheng (780-841) and T'ou-tzu Ta-t'ung (819-914). In turn, Yün-yen T'an-sheng transmitted the Dharma to Tung-shan Liang-chieh. Therefore, the authenticity of the Ts'ao-tung sect's connection with the Ch'an sect is clear and unquestionable.

Inquiry into Matching Halves is held in great regard by the Ts'ao-tung sect. The wisdom of Shih-t'ou's work was drawn upon extensively by Ts'ao-tung teachers, and they made *Inquiry into Matching Halves* more comprehensible to disciples. In Japanese Buddhist compilations, *Inquiry into Matching Halves* and *Song of the Precious Mirror Samadhi* are often grouped together in order to introduce the philosophy of the Soto sect. However, in my experience, I have yet to find any book which has expounded *Inquiry into Matching Halves* clearly.

Today in Taiwan there are few people who expound the teachings of these two Buddhist works. Since I am a Dharma descendant of the Ts'ao-tung lineage, I feel it is my responsibility to transmit Ts'ao-tung Dharma to my disciples and students. Part of that responsibilty includes explaining these important texts. I introduced these two Buddhist works in the Ch'an Meditation Center's Wednesday Dharma Class. Generally, I do not talk about Buddhist philosophy during intensive Ch'an retreats; instead I emphasize methods of practice. In the Wednesday Dharma Class, I talk about Buddhist philosophy as well as methods of practice. *Inquiry into Matching Halves* and *Song of the Precious Mirror Samadhi* are ideal texts for such a class.

In truth, the original Chinese versions of these two articles are extremely difficult to understand. Translating them into English was also no easy task. Both of these articles, along with brief biographies of their authors, already exist in *Poetry of Enlightenment.* In this book I offer in-depth commentaries on each text. My commentaries are based on my understanding of the texts, the Patriarchs who wrote them, and my experience derived from using their methods of practice. Since I am neither Shih-t'ou nor Tung-shan, I am sure that I have not fully and clearly explained the meaning of their works. They are difficult texts to penetrate. Questions arose constantly during the translation, explication, and even the editing of these texts. The more questions I was asked to explain, the clearer the text became. I am happy that the project is completed.

To my knowledge, there are no English commentaries on these Ts'ao-tung texts. I also believe there are no other English translations of the *Song of the Precious Mirror Samadhi*; there may be one English translation of *Inquiry into Matching Halves*. Of course, I may be wrong. My intention is that, with this book, these important Buddhist works may become known to English readers and more understandable to Buddhist practitioners. In reading this book, I hope followers of Buddhism will gain a better understand of the philosophy and methods of practice of Ts'ao-tung Ch'an. For many, it may be the first introduction to the teachings of this sect.

I would like to add that these commentaries are not scholarly treatises. The philosphy is intended for all sincere followers of Buddhism; the explanation of methods of practice are meant to inspire practice, not research. I have experience in doing research and writing academic treatises, but in this case, I leave it for someone else. I hope this small book will lead to more and better books on this subject.

Acknowledgements

I wish to sincerely thank everyone responsible for the creation of this book: Ming Yee Wang and Pei-gwang Dowiat, who expertly translated my often confusing lectures into English; Dorothy Weiner and Nancy Makso, who patiently transcribed the lectures; Chris Marano, who edited the bulk of the commentary and who was quite diligent in preparing the book efficiently; Harry Miller, who helped Chris enormously in his efforts to make the text understandable and palatable to readers; Stuart Lachs, who offered valuable criticism and knowledgable opinion about many of the concepts and the overall tone of the book; Jonathan Bardin and, again, Nancy Makso, who copy-edited and proof-read; and Page Simon, who designed this book and its cover; and Trish Ing, who supervised all phases of the book. I also wish to thank all members of the Wednesday Dharma Class. If not for them, this book would not exist.

INQUIRY INTO
MATCHING HALVES

by Shih-t'ou Hsi-ch'ien (700-790)

The mind of the great Indian immortal
Was esoterically transmitted from West to East.
The capacity of people may be dull or sharp,
But there are no Northern and Southern Patriarchs
     in the Tao.
The spiritual source is bright and pure,
Branching out and secretly flowing forth.
Attachment to phenomenon has always been confusion,
Yet union with principle is not enlightenment.
Every (Dharma) door includes all realms,
Some mutually interact, others do not.
Reaction increases mutual involvement;
There should be no reliance on abiding in one place.
From original form comes shapes and images;
From primal sound comes pleasures and pains.
In obscurity, words of the high and middle (paths)
     are in accord;
In lucidity, expressions of purity and muddiness are
     apparent.
The four great elements return to their own nature
As a child finds its mother.
Fire burns, wind moves and shakes,
Water moistens, earth solidifies.
Eyes – forms, ears – sounds,
Nose – odors, tongue – salt and sour.

In accordance with each dharma,
The root gives rise to separate leaves.
Roots and branches must return to basic principle;
"Honorable" and "lowly" are merely words.
In the midst of brightness there is darkness;
Do not take darkness as darkness.
In the midst of darkness there is brightness;
Do not take brightness as brightness.
Brightness and darkness correspond,
Like one step following another.
All things have their own function
Depending on their use and location.
Phenomena stores, seals, covers, combines.
Principle yields to the arrow, the sword's edge,
*   the stick.*
Received teachings must be reconciled with
*   basic principle;*
Do not establish your own rules.
Using your eyes, the path is lost.
Using your feet, how can you know the road?
Moving forward there is no near or far;
Confusion creates mountains and rivers of obstructions.
I implore those who investigate the mysterious:
Do not waste your time!

Introduction

Before I begin my commentary on *Inquiry Into Matching Halves*, I would like to speak briefly on the life and accomplishments of its author, Shih-t'ou Hsi-ch'ien (700-790). who lived during the T'ang dynasty (618-907). He became a monk at the age of thirteen, and began practicing with the Sixth Patriarch, Hui-neng (638-713). However, Hui-neng died soon after, and Shih-t'ou was directed to study with an important disciple of the Sixth Patriarch – Ch'ing-yüan Hsing-ssu (660-740).

The Ts'ao-tung sect, which places great importance on *Inquiry Into Matching Halves*, traces its origins to Shih-t'ou Hsi-ch'ien. However, it is not Shih-tou, but rather two of his Dharma descendants, who are credited with creating the Ts'ao-tung sect.

Shih-t'ou Hsi-ch'ien's Dharma lineage proceeds as follows: Yao-shan Wei-yen (745-828), Yun-yen T'an-sheng (780-841), Tung-shan Liang-chieh (807-869), Ts'ao-shan Pen-chi (840-901). Tung-shan Liang-chieh and Ts'ao-shan Pen-chi are the recognized founders of the Ts'ao-tung sect, and in fact, the Ts'ao-tung sect derives its name from the surnames of these two patriarchs.

The Chinese rendering of Shih-t'ou's poem title is *Ts'an T'ung Ch'i.* The title's origins date back to the Eastern Han dynasty (25-220), long before Shih-tou's lifetime. *Ts'an T'ung Ch'i* is the title of another book, written by a Taoist named Wei Po Yang. The Taoist work delineated esoteric practices that could help one to gain immortality or transform oneself into a deity. But why would Shih-t'ou adopt the title of a Taoist work for his poem? When Buddhism migrated to China, Sakyamuni Buddha was given a Taoist appelation – The Perfectly Enlightened Highest Deity – in order to form a connection between Buddhist teaching and the Taoist tradition. By adopting the Taoist title, Shih-t'ou made a metaphoric connection between becoming a deity and becoming a Buddha. Practice, Shih-t'ou advises, will lead to Buddhahood or the state of a "Perfectly Enlightened Deities." Furthermore, there is also an allusion within the title to the achievement of Buddhahood through the practice of *dhyana*, which is similar to some Taoist practices.

The title consists of three characters. *Ch'i* means contract. When two people come to an agreement in order to achieve a goal, this contract is called *ch'i*. People who marry in court must affirm their agreement; the affirmation is called *ch'i*.

T'ung means common. In this poem's title, "common" refers to all the Buddhas throughout space and time. The phrase *t'ung chi* implies that this affirmation is not merely an agreement between two people. Rather, all the Buddhas affirm that, in order to reach Buddhahood, one must follow the path described by the teachings of this poem.

Ts'an can either be translated as "work" or as "investigation." One must make an effort to investigate the meaning of things. The poem's title refers to one investigating the meaning of *t'ung ch'i*, or that which is affirmed by the Buddhas. It is the same kind of questioning one encounters in *kung-an* and *hua-t'ou* practice. In fact, many *kung-ans* are derived from the teachings of *Ts'an T'ung Ch'i* and the Ts'ao-tung sect. For example, one famous *kung-an* asks: What is the meaning of Bodhidharma coming from the West? Of course, you cannot answer that he left India to bring the Dharma to China, because that answer would be based on intellectual reasoning. Underlying the question is something that cannot be explained in words or language. When a person investigates this particular *kung-an*, he is, in fact, trying to reveal that which is affirmed by all Buddhas. It is an instance of *ts'an t'ung ch'i.*

Two terms in this verse – *ming* and *an* – are of great importance. Literally, they mean "brightness" and "darkness." In later writings of the Ts'ao-tung sect, authors often referred to paired concepts such as "center and off-center," or "king and subordinate." One of the paired terms – brightness, center, or king – represents something that is primary; and the other term – darkness, off-center, or subordinate – represents something that is auxiliary. These paired opposites were used by Ts'ao-tung masters to help explain the experience of practice. For expedience, Ts'ao-tung masters divided the experience of enlightenment into five progressive levels. Using paired opposites to help explain the five levels of the Ts'ao-tung sect originated with Shih-tou's terms, *ming* and *an.*

Shih-t'ou Hsi-Ch'ien had tremendous impact on

the Ch'an sect, especially the Ts'ao-tung sect. Since *Ts'an T'ung Ch'i* contains his fundamental ideas, it is worthwhile to discuss the meaning of his poem. On the other hand, the concepts in *Ts'an T'ung Ch'i* are difficult to understand, and at this time there are no English commentaries on Shih-tou's poem. I hope that more and better commentaries on *Inquiry Into Matching Halves* will follow. For now this commentary may be helpful to the reader.

Inquiry Into Matching Halves

The mind of the great Indian immortal
Was esoterically transmitted from West to
*   East.*

The great Indian immortal refers to Sakyamuni Buddha. Sakyamuni did not bring Buddhism from the West to the East. Historically, Bodhidharma is credited with introducing Buddhism to China, but these two lines of verse are not referring to Bodhidharma either. The poem speaks of the mind of the Buddha, not the Buddha himself. The mind that was esoterically transmitted from West to East refers to the wisdom of a perfectly enlightened being. In technical terms, it is called the "Dharma door of the mind-ground."

Sakyamuni Buddha made a vow to sit under the *Bodhi* tree until he reached ultimate enlightenment. It is said that his mind brightened when he revealed his true nature. The mind brightens when all vexations are terminated. If a practitioner accomplishes this, he will see the true nature of all dharmas. This true nature goes by many names: it is sometimes called Dharma nature; before one is enlightened, it is also called Buddha-nature, and after one is enlightened, it is called Buddha's wisdom.

Before sentient beings become enlightened, they do not know what the mind of Buddha is like or where it is. Only those who penetrate their true nature will be aware of the true mind. For this reason, it is said that the mind, or wisdom, of the Buddha is transmitted secretly, esoterically.

Those who are not enlightened cannot see this mind, and Buddha cannot show it to them. A practitioner must come to his own understanding. Buddha can only offer Dharma; he cannot transform anyone into a Buddha. If Buddha himself cannot reveal this mind to us, then how can the patriarchs after Buddha do so? Enlightenment must be attained by the practitioner.

However, although it seems contradictory, those who are enlightened understand that Buddha has clearly and completely transmitted his wisdom to them. In other words, one can say that Buddha reveals his mind to those who attain thorough enlightenment. Completely enlightened people also clearly perceive that this mind has been transmitted from the West (India) to the East by generations of patriarchs. Shih-t'ou uses the term "patriarch" to describe completely enlightened people, who see clearly what the mind is.

Another name for this true mind is the Right Dharma Eye Storehouse. Every dharma comes from this storehouse, but only those who are enlightened – those who have opened their eyes – can see the Dharma Storehouse. When the mind is transmitted from patriarch to patriarch, it is sometimes called the "Transmission of the Dharma," or "Giving of the Dharma," but it is formally called the "Giving of the Dharma Storehouse." Likewise, the record of the genealogy of patriarchs has a special name. Translated from Chinese, it is called the "Record of Causes and Conditions for the Giving of the Dharma Storehouse."

Of course, transmission of the Dharma Storehouse from patriarch to patriarch – from master to disciple – is no secret. To the donor and recipient, the transmision of the Dharma Storehouse is clear and obvious. However, sentient beings who are not enlightened have no idea what is transpiring. For the unenlightened, the transmission of the Dharma Storehouse is a secret, and until they are enlightened, it will remain a mystery.

> *The capacity of people may be dull or*
> *sharp,*
> *But there are no Northern and Southern*
> *Patriarchs in the Tao.*

Even though the karmic roots, or karmic capacities, of unenlightened sentient beings vary, there is no distinction among patriarchs from the South, East, North, or West.

It is true that people have different karmic roots. If you practice or study Buddhadharma – even if you think you practice poorly – you should be happy. It is rare that one encounters, accepts and practices Buddhadharma; it means that you have a deep karmic connection with the Dharma. However, having a deep karmic connection with the Dharma is not the same as having dull or sharp karmic roots. People who encounter the Dharma may have equivalent karmic affinity with the Dharma, but some may have sharp roots and others, dull roots. Those with sharp roots can cut through vexations quicker than those with dull roots.

Consider a ball made of iron. Although it may be heavy, it may also be too dull to rip through a paper bag. Therefore, the ball can remain hidden. The practice of a person with deep, but dull, karmic roots can be likened to an iron ball in a bag. Though the practitioner's connection with the Dharma is deep, his capacity for practice is dull, and he may not be able to quickly cut through his vexations. However, a person with sharp karmic roots is equivalent to an iron sword. With the slightest pressure, the sword can cut through the bag.

People who practice a long time, yet are unable to reveal their true nature, must recognize and admit to themselves that they have dull karmic roots. However, they should not despair. Yes, their karmic roots may be dull, but their karmic connection with the Dharma is deep. People like this must persist in their practice, continuously polishing and hammering their iron ball, until they fashion a sharp edge that can puncture the walls of their karmic obstructions. Only then will the sword become visible.

Legend has it that Sakyamuni Buddha's son, Rahula, remained in the womb of Yasutara – Sakyamuni's wife – for six years. Yasutara became pregnant while Sakyamuni still lived in his father's palace, but she did not give birth to Rahula until Sakyamuni attained complete enlightenment. People in the palace accused Yasutara of committing adultery, and they condemned her to death. She said, "I know I am innocent. To prove it to you, I will undergo a test. Place a stone in the water, and I will stand with my child on the stone. If we sink, it means I'm guilty, and it's appropriate that we drown. If we float, it means I'm innocent." Of course, mother, child, and stone did not sink, and she was vindicated.

Sakyamuni Buddha explained why Rahula stayed in the mother's womb for so long. Lifetimes before, Rahula saw a snake slither into a hole. He blocked the hole and trap the snake. After six days, Rahula removed the stone and let the snake go free. As a consequence of that action, Rahula remained in his mother's womb for six years.

In this story, Buddha recounted only one of Rahula's past actions. It would be impossible to keep track of all the bad karma we have accumulated over countless lifetimes from evil actions directed toward other sentient beings. Our bad karma creates obstacles on the path of practice in this lifetime. Just as Rahula could not leave his mother's womb, our wisdom cannot break through our karmic obstructions. As long as we are obstructed by our previous actions, our karmic roots will remain dull, regardless of how deep our karmic affinity with the Dharma may be.

In order to make progress, people must openly face their karmic obstructions and accept the consequences of previous actions. They must be persistent and determined in their practice, in this lifetime and in lifetimes to come.

People who feel they have dull karmic roots need not feel helpless. Likewise, they have no reason to envy people with sharp karmic roots. There are individuals who simultaneously have a deep karmic affinity with the Dharma and sharp karmic roots. They make quick progress in a short time and do not regress on the path of practice. These people have deep enlightenment experiences; that is, with one experience they eradicate all vexations and become thoroughly enlightened. Such people are extremely rare. More often, people who make quick progress in their practice (because they do not have many karmic obstructions) do not have deep karmic affinity with the Dharma. Their karmic roots are sharp – they see their self-nature after practicing for a short time – but, because they do not have a deep connection with the Dharma, the benefits derived from the enlightenment are weak and short-lived. They are not capable of generating enduring power from their experience, and because they do not continue to practice diligently afterwards, whatever benefit they get quickly disappears.

Ch'an masters say that before one is enlightened, one must practice diligently and gravely as if one's parents had just died. However, after one is enlightened, one has to practice doubly hard, with an even graver mentality, as if one's parents had died twice. Why is this? Before you are enlightened, you are in a pitiable condition. You do not know where you come from; you do not know where you are going; you do not know who you are. There is no other choice but to practice hard and earnestly to discover the answers to these questions. People who are enlightened know where they come from and where they are going. However, a person without deep karmic affinity with the Dharma who sees his self-nature must be careful, because he can easily regress or digress from the correct practice. It is as if he were walking on a narrow, treacherous path. If he is careless, he can lose his way and find himself in a strange place again. After an enlightenment experience, it is necessary to keep practicing diligently, until one reaches a wide, safe path.

The Tao that Shih-t'ou refers to in the couplet refers to the Buddha mind as well as to the path that leads to the Buddha mind. Practitioners who are not yet enlightened do not know where they are or where they are going. For such people, the Tao refers to the path that leads to Buddhahood. After seeing their self-nature, practitioners know where they are and where they are going. However, they must still traverse the path of practice, so it is necessary to continue speaking of the Tao. When a sentient being reaches Buddhahood, it is no longer necessary to speak of the Tao. We sometimes refer to the Tao as the Buddha path, but it is only for the benefit of sentient beings who have not reached Buddhahood that we need such a term. For Buddhas, there is no Buddha path.

We must understand that seeing into one's nature, or experiencing enlightenment, does not necessarily mean one is permanently enlightened. Enlightenment is a momentary flash when a person sees his true nature – the nature of no self. According to the Ch'an historical record, there have been a few monks who, in one enlightenment experience, became thoroughly enlightened; Masters Yang-shan (807-883) and Wei-shan (771-853) of the T'ang dynasty are two such individuals. They are Ch'an masters of the highest order. There have not been many such instances. More often, one enlightenment is not enough. A practitioner needs to experience many enlightenments; some will be shallow, some deep. One Sung dynasty master said he had more than thirty deep enlightenments and uncountable shallow enlightenments in his lifetime. A wise master will rarely allow students to teach after an initial enlightenment experience. They still need to practice diligently.

The Ts'ao-tung sect speaks of five levels of progress along the Buddha path. Later, masters of the Ming dynasty spoke of three barriers to practice. Passing through the first barrier is equivalent to having an initial enlightenment experience. It is like passing over a threshold. A master may affirm your experience, but it is doubtful he will allow you to teach others. There is still much work to be done.

The next level is called the "multiple barrier." During this stage, a practitioner will have several enlightenments. Usually, experiences will be progressively stronger, and the power derived from the experience will last longer.

When I speak of power and benefits, I refer to the amount and number of vexations that disappear. An enlightenment experience may only last an instant. In that instant a practitioner will understand the illusory nature of his vexations, and for a while his attachments and vexations, which stem from greed, hatred, ignorance, doubt and arrogance, will disappear. Depending on the depth and strength of his enlightenment experience, his vexations may return right away, or they may not return for a longer period of time. With thorough enlightenment, vexations never return.

The third level is called the "prison barrier." A practitioner who breaks through the third barrier breaks through the bonds of Samsara. Such a person has attained liberation – thorough enlightenment – and vexations will not return. It still does not mean that practice is over. A liberated practitioner can teach others, but he can practice as well, in order to accumulate more wisdom and merit. This level is equivalent to the tenth picture of the *Ten Ox Herding Pictures.*

It is possible for a person to break through the prison barrier with his first enlightenment experience, but more often a person must pass through the multiple barrier stage. Practitioners who pass through all three barriers in one enlightenment have deep and sharp karmic roots. They possess a sharp, iron sword. In the early days of Ch'an, monks and nuns would not get permission to teach until they had passed through the prison barrier, but things are different today. Some practitioners may be given permission to teach while they are still on the second, or even the first, level.

People who have had an initial enlightenment experience should realize that they have not reached ultimate enlightenment. They should seek the guidance of a master, or study the sutras. If no masters are available, then it is permissable for them to teach, but they must be cautious. They must understand that there are still problems to work out. Their experience is shallow, so they must be careful not to mislead their followers. They should let their students know that they are not deeply enlightened. If followers mistake their teachers for thoroughly enlightened beings, they may later be let down by the teachers' words or actions. That would not be fair to the followers, and it would be an injustice to the Dharma. Teachers who have had only an initial enlightenment must be humble. Most of all, they must continue to practice.

One can liken such a teacher to a coach. A coach may not be an outstanding athlete, but he may have the ability to guide others to become outstanding athletes. I often say that I am like a one-legged man surrounded by no-legged students. I cannot move quickly, but at least I can get around. I know having one leg is not good enough, that it is possible to have two legs. With such knowledge, I can teach no-legged students to grow both legs.

I am often asked if it is possible for an intiial enlightenment to fade such that a practitioner forgets his experience and stops practicing. It is not the flash of experience that fades, but the power derived from that experience which fades. If the enlightenment is genuine, then a person will clearly see what his true nature is, and he will work doubly hard in his practice, because his faith and power of practice will have increased. If a person claims to have been enlightened, then be on your guard. If he does not practice and acts in immoral ways, then more than likely he did not have a genuine experience. Of course, it is possible that certain karmic conditions will prevent a practitioner from practicing after an initial enlightenment, but this is the exception to the rule. Furthermore, the power derived from practice is not magical; it is not an entity or force that pushes one along in one's practice. Power is the absence of greed, hatred, ignorance, arrogance and doubt. When power fades, these vexations return. That should be enough impetus for a person to continue to practice. Once one has experienced life without these vexations, even if only for a moment, one should have the faith and determination to practice until vexations eventually lessen and disappear forever.

> *The spiritual source is bright and pure,*
> *Branching out and secretly flowing forth.*

The spiritual source refers to the potential for Buddhahood, or the seed of Buddhahood, that is within all of us. It is called Buddha-nature. The spiritual source can also be described as the undefiled master that is within each of us.

The Chinese character which is translated as "spiritual source" has other connotations. It alludes to something that is free, yet soft, like a gentle, unobstructed light that has the power of illumination. The same Chinese characters are sometimes used to describe moonlight; moonlight is considered gentle and undefiled. Hence, the spiritual source is completely unobstructed, bright, pure and clear.

From an enlightened person's point of view, the spiritual source is pure and unmoving. It has no power because no power is needed; there is only Suchness. For ordinary sentient beings, however, the spiritual source has the power of illumination, because they are in the darkness of ignorance and they need the power of illumination to escape that darkness. When the spiritual source displays this power of illumination, it is called wisdom.

The spiritual source is within each sentient being and common to all sentient beings. Before enlightenment, however, sentient beings are obstructed by their ignorance, and their spiritual source is covered by vexation. Each sentient being is unique. One can say that each sentient being is a different branch of the flowing spiritual source that is common to all.

From Buddha's point of view, the spiritual source is common to everyone. In other words, the pure, undefiled light of Buddha-nature is everywhere equal. But sentient beings are not enlightened, and they see themselves immersed in darkness, apart from the spiritual source. They see the light of the spiritual source as wisdom, and the darkness around them as vexation. Each person is unique in that he has his own vexations. Sentient beings perceive different levels of darkness depending on how deeply they are immersed in vexation. To Buddha, there is really no difference between wisdom and vexation. However, Buddha responds instantly and unconditionally to the needs of sentient beings.

Sentient beings, as they branch from this common

spiritual source, meander in innumerable directions. Depending on their vexations and karma, sentient beings flow to and from different points along different paths, filling the six realms in the endless cycle of Samsara.

The first line of this couplet refers to light, or brightness. The second line refers to darkness. Lightness represents enlightenment, and darkness represents vexation, or the condition of sentient beings before enlightenment. In this couplet, brightness and darkness are described as being separate and distinct. Brightness is brightness. Darkness is darkness. The distinction is quite clear. However, the distinction between brightness and darkness is an expedient teaching of Buddhadharma, taught for the benefit of ordinary sentient beings.

> *Attachment to phenomenon has always*
> *been confusion,*
> *Yet union with principle is not enlightenment.*

This couplet reflects back to the previous two lines. I said that brightness and darkness are separate and distinct. That, however, stems from teachings of certain doctrinal schools of Buddhism. It is not the highest Dharma. This couplet reminds us that viewing brightness and darkness as distinct entities is not ultimate Buddhadharma.

If one distinguishes between brightness and darkness, vexation and wisdom, or Samsara and Nirvana, that is discrimination. Discrimination stems from ignorance. If you discriminate – that is, if you cling to differences among phenomena and make distinctions based on attachment – then you are not enlightened. You are still deluded and cling to a point of view. These are characteristics of ordinary sentient beings, not enlightened beings.

The first line of the couplet explains that you are still confused or deluded if you attach to the phenomena that emanate from brightness and darkness.

The second line of the couplet warns that being in union with the principle is not enlightenment either. Here, "principle" refers to perceiving brightness and darkness as being one and the same. If a person does not make distinctions between brightness and darkness, then he is in accordance with, or in union with, the principle. But this is not enlightenment.

Why is being in accordance with the principle not enlightenment? Accordance with the principle can be considered worldly enlightenment. It refers to a one-mind state. Although it is a powerful and worthwhile experience, it is not enlightenment in the Buddhist sense, because there is still a self involved. We can call it "Great Self," or *atman* – Shih-t'ou refers to it as the "principle" – but it is not enlightenment. It does not liberate one from Samsara.

People who hold onto the principle as the ultimate truth will likely believe in a fundamental nature that is real, unchanging and eternal. A basic tenet of Buddhism states, however, that there is no unchanging, eternal nature. Emptiness underlies existence. Clinging to an eternal, universal, unchanging principle is, in fact, holding onto a Great Self.

> *Every (Dharma) door includes all realms,*
> *Some mutually interact, others do not.*

We are all familiar with the T'ai-chi symbol of yin and yang – a circle that is half white and half black. On the one hand, yin and yang are separate and distinct. On the other hand, yin and yang are part of the same circle. Although Shih-t'ou does not speak of the T'ai-chi symbol, he does use the symbols of brightness and darkness in a similar manner. Yin and yang and brightness and darkness are polarities or opposite elements which mutually interact.

Before I continue with an explanation of this verse, I wish to explain two Buddhist terms, namely nature and dharma, because it will help to make clear much of what I will discuss from this point onward. In Buddhism, the word "nature" has several meanings. Sometimes we take nature as the essential way things are, as in self-nature. Although we say that we seek our self-nature, there really is no such thing. Self-nature is at bottom nothing but a dharma. Dharmas, whether they are physical or mental, do not have a permanent, unchanging existence. Therefore, there is no self-nature. On the other hand, when dharmas arise from causes and conditions, they do have their own particular "natures." Here, nature refers to characteristics. A dharma, whether it is physical or mental, has defining qualities, a position, and also a path on which it travels (arises and perishes). Each dharma abides in its own realm. The interaction of dharmas, with their unique characteristics, paths and realms, are what constitute the universe (*dharmadhatu*). Furthermore, we should make a distinction between Dharma and dharma. Dharma with an upper case "D" refers to the body of teachings, methods and principles of Buddhism. Dharma with a lower case "d" refers to any and all phenomena. It should be pointed out that the Dharma is, in fact, a collection of dharmas.

If you look at the English translation of the first line of this couplet, you will notice that "door" is emphasized while "dharma" is enclosed in parentheses. Actually, "dharma" should be emphasized. "Door" need not be mentioned. Every dharma includes all realms. In essence, every dharma is part of and connected to every other dharma. What does this mean?

The Ts'ao-tung sect often borrows terminology and symbols from the *I Ching*. In the *I Ching*, yin, or darkness, is represented by a broken line, and yang, or brightness, is represented by an unbroken line. These lines are combined in sets of six called hexagrams. According to the *I Ching*, the sixty-four possible hexagrams represent, and can be used to interpret, all phenomena. We are discussing Buddhism, not Taoism or the *I Ching*, but one point is common to all three beliefs. Each phenomenon, or dharma, no matter how large or small, is connected to and part of all other phenomena.

I said that all dharmas, or phenomena, are connected to and part of everything that emanates from the interaction of opposite elements symbolized by yin and yang. All dharmas arise from causes and conditions, which are ever-changing and mutually interdependent. In fact, without causes and conditions, and without the interaction of yin and yang, dharmas cannot arise. For something to exist, it must be compared to something that does not exist. Existence can be recognized only in contrast to non-existence. Furthermore, the comparison of existence and non-existence is, itself, an interaction of yin and yang.

When opposite elements come together, it does not mean that they will stay together. The yin-yang circle gives the impression of fluidity, of an ever-changing nature. Phenomena arise, change, and disappear with the incessant flux of causes and conditions. Phenomena will continuously arise and come into contact with other phenomena. Still, no matter how much interplay or change occurs, all phenomena are part of the totality represented by yin and yang, or existence and non-existence. In essence, all things change, but on a larger scale, nothing moves. Yin and yang are still part of the same circle. Every dharma interacts with every other dharma. Each individual dharma encompasses every other dharma. Each dharma encompasses the totality represented by yin and yang, and at the same time, each dharma emanates from the interaction of yin and yang.

We cannot view each dharma as an isolated event, an isolated interaction of opposite elements. The *I Ching* emphasizes that yin and yang evolve into innumerable phenomena. Each dharma, which arises from the inter-action of yin and yang, constantly interacts with other dharmas, which are also products of yin and yang. Additionally, the interaction between each dharma is also a product of yin and yang. Each dharma is not only connected to every other dharma, it also includes all dharmas, all realms, all of totality. The *Avatamsaka Sutra* says that a single grain of sand contains innumerable sutras. One grain of sand contains all Buddhadharma.

Buddhism says that dharmas arise from causes and conditions. Since dharmas arise from causes and conditions, they do not have unchanging natures. There-fore, they are empty. It is precisely because dharmas arise from causes and conditions that we can recognize their empty nature. Conversely, it is because of empti-ness that dharmas can arise from causes and conditions. If dharmas were not fundamentally empty, then they would be solid, enduring, unchanging, and they would not arise and perish as a result of the coming together of causes and conditions. In effect, dharmas (which arise from causes and conditions) and emptiness are mutually interdependent. They are cause and consequence for one another.

Emptiness is represented by brightness. It is the spiritual source. The dharmas arising from causes and conditions are represented by darkness – darkness be-cause dharmas have obstructions. Dharmas are in the realm of existence, and obstruction and attachment are part of existence. Emptiness is bright because no attachment or obstructions exist. Emptiness is also called the principle, and the dharmas arising from causes and conditions are called phenomena.

I said that every dharma contains *yin* and yang. Using Shih-t'ou's terminology, every dharma contains both brightness and darkness, or emptiness and non-emptiness. Ordinary sentient beings are attached to and only see the non-empty aspect of dharmas. We see only the dharmas, only the phenomena, not the underlying causes and conditions. Enlightened ones, however, sees both the dharmas and the fundamental emptiness from which they arise. Therefore, they do not become attached to phenomena.

Ordinary sentient beings are unable to recognize that every dharma includes all realms. Enlightened sentient beings perceive dharmas arising from causes and conditions. They see that dharmas arise from emptiness. Therefore, they recognize that each dharma includes all other dharmas, and in turn, each dharma is encompassed by all other dharmas.

The second line of the couplet says that dharmas interact, yet they do not interact. Interaction means that phenomena are related. For instance, people in the same room breathe each other's air. They are related. It does not mean that each of us breathes all the air, but over an extended period of time, that may happen. Extending the analogy, one can say that each person is related to all of *dharmadhatu* – the entire universe. It may be difficult for you to understand or accept this. All dharmas are related and interact. However, the manifestation or effect of that relationship may not become evident for aeons. You and I are talking right now. The effect of our interaction seems to be immediate. At the same time, you are also interacting with dharma on the other side of the universe, but it may not become apparent for a long time to come, or it may never become apparent. This is what the line, "some dharmas interact" means.

What does it mean when the stanza says, "others [dharmas] do not [interact]."? This can be understood on two levels. One level refers to the person who has reached the "one-mind" state. To him, there is no interaction –7 there is no coming in or going out, there is no shifting. All is contained within the "one." Since all is contained in the "one," nothing really happens.

The second level refers to a person who has attained the state of "no-self." An enlightened being is aware of all changes, relationships and interactions, but since he has no self, he attaches to none of it and is moved by none of it.

> *Reaction increases mutual involvement;*
> *There should be no reliance on abiding in*
> *one place.*

Not only do phenomena mutually interact in the present moment, the process continues successively and uninterrupted, interaction after interaction, developing and expanding without limit. One dharma interacts with innumerable other dharmas, and those dharmas, in turn, interact with the "original" dharma. Therefore, it is said that one dharma leads to, or gives rise to, all dharmas. To put it another way, one dharma contains all dharmas. It does not mean that there is an original dharma from which all other dharmas spring. Although one dharma contains all other dharmas, you cannot hold onto that one dharma and forget the rest.

The term "mutually interacting" refers to all dharmas. One dharma leads to other dharmas, but at the same time, each of the other dharmas leads back to the first dharma. There is no first or special dharma. Every dharma contains all dharmas and leads to all dharmas. If this were not true, then we could not speak of unlimited dharmas arising from a single dharma.

If, in your practice, you enter enlightenment through one method – one Dharma door – in fact, you enter all Dharma doors. However, you cannot say that only one Dharma door is necessary and ignore the other Dharma doors. For example, there are four doors that open into the Ch'an hall. No matter which door I choose, it will lead into this hall, but it does not mean that only one door is necessary. Each door is an access to another part of the building. All four doors are necessary, and lead in different directions, yet they are all related.

Although one dharma incorporates in its essence all other dharmas, each of the other dharmas has its own position. It is not as if every dharma is in the same space and time as the arbitrary dharma that I choose to say contains all dharmas. Each dharma has its own position, its own point of view, its own perspective. Unity, then, does not mean that there are no differences between dharmas, or phenomena, but rather, that all differences are incorporated, or contained, within each dharma. Only an enlightened person truly understands these ideas. An enlightened person sees every dharma as it is, without discrimination and attachment. One dharma is not different from any other dharma. In seeing one dharma, an enlightened person sees all dharmas. But he also sees that each dharma has its own position.

Once, master Yang-shan asked his master, Wei-shan, "If millions of myriads of phenomena were to arise simultaneously, what would you do?" His master replied, "Green is not yellow, long is not short. Each dharma abides in its own position. It has nothing to do with me." Innumerable dharmas exist, each with its unique position and characteristics, but they have no influence or effect on an enlightened person. In other words, an enlightened person interacts spontaneously with phenomena, yet he is not attached to dharma. He is subject to sickness and death, but he is not attached to the suffering of sickness and death. In this way, he moves freely through the world, interacting with sentient beings and the environment, yet he clings to nothing.

Unenlightened people can only vaguely understand the true meaning of the phrase, "the mutual interaction of dharmas," because they use their intellect, and therefore, they misinterpret the essence of Buddhist principles. For instance, I have said that one dharma contains all dharmas. However, if, with your reasoning power, you think that within each dharma is the *potential* for every other dharma to arise, then you have misunderstood the teaching. In fact, one dharma already contains all dharmas, in this and every moment. The Ch'an sect has a saying: "A single thought contains the Ten Dharma Realms." If you read this line and think, "Because I think of this, therefore I can think of that, and then that, and so on, until, potentially, I will understand the Ten Dharma Realms," then you have misunderstood the phrase. Actually, your single thought, right now, contains all Ten Dharma Realms. A single thought contains you, your self-nature, everyone in this room, everyone you know, all your dreams and memories, the environment, the universe.

When I say one dharma contains all dharmas, you may think I use the word "contain" in a metaphorical sense. Actually, I use the word literally. One thought, no matter how small it may seem, spatially and temporally contains the Ten Dharma Realms. This is so because true nature, or Buddha-nature, is the same for all sentient beings, all worlds, all heavens, all hells, all Buddhas.

Therefore, one dharma, whether it is a mental dharma (consciousness) or a physical dharma (form), includes all dharmas.

The *Avatamsaka Sutra* says that all Buddhas in the three times and ten directions turn the Great Dharma Wheel on the tip of a fine strand of hair. It is not symbolic language. It is the literal truth. If I hold onto one thread of my robe, in fact I hold the entire robe. Likewise, since all dharmas have the same fundamental nature, in holding one I hold them all. It does not mean that I can get to all other dharmas, one by one, by holding onto the original dharma. It is not like a snowball rolling down a hill, amassing more snow as it descends. I do not amass dharmas by holding onto one dharma. Rather, in holding this dharma, I instantaneously hold all dharmas.

Dharmas arise from causes and conditions. One dharma is connected, through causes and conditions, to all other dharmas. Therefore, if you hold one dharma, you are in direct contact with all other dharmas.

> *From original form comes shapes and*
> *images;*
> *From primal sound comes pleasures and*
> *pains.*

Previously, I said that the phenomena of the world can be traced to the mutual interaction of yin and yang, or brightness and darkness. All phenomena are part of, and not separate from, form. Form refers to all material dharmas. Each form has a particular shape and image. Each form has unique characteristics. The first line of this couplet alludes to an ancient philosophical school (Kapila School) in India, which claims that all phenomena derive from the interaction and combination of numbers. Numbers, the school maintains, are the fundamental basis of form and phenomena in the universe.

The second line of the couplet refers to another Indian philosophical school (Vyakarana School), which maintains that the universe is based on sound – the universe originally comes from sound and will eventually return to sound. Because people are different, they hear different sounds, which in turn triggers feelings of pleasure and pain. Furthermore, sound develops into language, and from language comes more complex feelings and perceptions – pleasure derived from flattery and compliments; pain derived from criticism and condemnation.

Originally there is unity, but from unity arises differentiation. The first line refers to differentiation in terms of form and shape. The second line refers to differentiation in terms of sound.

Shih-t'ou does not speak of fundamental form and sound strictly from a theoretical standpoint. He speaks from direct, spiritual experience. Superficially speaking, one can say that, because sentient beings are unique, people hear different sounds, and these sounds in turn lead to sensations of pain and pleasure. All of these ideas are true. However, there is a deeper, more direct experience, which corresponds to the experience of *samadhi.*

The Ch'an school sometimes speaks of four stages of enlightenment. The first stage is called the "infinite realm of light and sound." "Light" refers to "form." The infinite light of the first stage of enlightenment is not light that ordinary people see. It is the light that exists before the beginning of the universe, before differentiation. It has no obstructions. In contrast, the light we see is the light of differentiated phenomena, and is quite limited in its scope. The infinite sound that one hears in *samadhi* is not the sound ordinary people hear. The sounds we think we hear are only illusions. They are quite different from the infinite sound that exists before differentiation.

From the original, unchanging, united light and sound come all the differentiated phenomena of form, shape and sound. However, to understand this, one must be at the first stage of enlightenment. In writing this couplet, Shih-t'ou has grouped together all the philosophical and spiritual schools which speak of reality and phenomena in terms of form and sound – not only the two Indian philosphical schools, but all practices which rely on mantras, names, or numbers. Shih-t'ou does not condemn the teachings of these traditions. He recognizes the benefits of such practice. He does not disclaim that differentiation comes from and returns to unity. The experience of Ch'an, however, is beyond the level attainable through these techniques.

If you abide in the realm of infinite light and form, then you still have attachments, and you still reside in the realm of form. Even the formless realms are not Ch'an. Residing in the formless realms of deep *samadhi*, one still clings, however subtly, to the idea of abiding in emptiness. A sense of self still exists. The emptiness of the formless realms of *samadhi* is different from Ch'an emptiness.

> *In obscurity, words of the high and middle*
> *(path) are in accord;*
> *In lucidity, expressions of purity or*
> *muddiness are apparent.*

The word "obscurity," sometimes translated as "hiddenness," refers to wisdom that is covered up. The word "lucidity," sometimes translated as "clarity," refers to wisdom manifest. For ordinary sentient beings, wisdom is hidden, or obscured, by vexation. Although it is hidden, wisdom is never separate from the "high (superior) and middling words." The high and middling words are the teachings of the Mahayana vehicle (Bodhisattva path) and the Hinayana vehicle (Liberation path). The lower path, which is not mentioned, encompasses the human and heavenly realms. In other words, even though wisdom is obscured when one is unenlightened, it is never separate from the enlightened states of the Mahayana and Hinayana paths.

The second line of the couplet explains that wisdom manifests in order to distinguish without attachment between that which is pure and that which is impure. Obscurity and lucidity, hiddenness and clarity, phenomena and principle, yin and yang, darkness and brightness, existence and emptiness – these are paired opposites that are commonly used by masters of the Ts'ao-tung sect in order to distinguish between the enlightened and unenlightened states. In this couplet, obscurity refers to existence, and lucidity to emptiness. But, as I have explained earlier, existence and emptiness are not separate and apart from one another.

Wisdom is obscured because ordinary sentient beings are moved by or attracted to phenomena – the environment. These phenomena do not move. The mind moves, and thereby, the environment moves. When the mind is in motion, wisdom is obscured. If the mind does not move, then phenomena are still. There is a famous story in the *Platform Sutra* which perfectly illustrates this concept. The Sixth Patriarch, Hui-neng, approached two monks who disagreed about a flag waving in the wind. One said the flag moved, and the other said it was the wind that moved. Hui-neng told them that it was their minds that were moving. The environment moves because our minds move.

The *Sutra of Complete Enlightenment* expounds on the same concept, but at a shallower level; one that is more easily understood by the intellect. The sutra says that when the clouds move in the night sky, it is as if the clouds are still and the moon is moving; likewise, when we sit in a boat floating downstream, it feels as if the riverbank is moving, not the boat. These analogies describe an already moving mind that is confused even further by illusory phenomena. On a deeper level, the mind of vexation creates new karma, which in turn leads to the movement of phenomena. Every phenomenon is a construct of the movement of our minds. Therefore, phenomena exist only because of the action of our minds. Understand that there is an objective existence. The chair I sit on does not appear out of thin air because my mind moves. But it is my moving mind that sees this physical mass and adds mental constructions – views it, perceives it, interprets it, gives meaning to it.

"Obscurity" refers to vexation, to sentient beings who are not enlightened, whether they practice or do not practice. This condition of obscurity is called *Tathagatagarbha*, or the storehouse of *Tathagata*. *Tathagata* means "Suchness." Although sentient beings are immersed in vexation, the *Tathagata* is stored within them. For this reason, all sentient beings have the potential to become arhats, Bodhisattvas and Buddhas.

We are in a "hidden" condition because we are sentient beings. We are *Tathagatagarbha* – Buddha-nature. It does not mean that we are Buddhas right now, or that we have ever been Buddhas. Rather, we have the potential to reveal our Buddha-nature. When we are in the realm of Samsara, we speak of *Tathagatagarbha*, because it has not yet been uncovered. After enlightenment, and once outside of Samsara, we speak of True Suchness. Because all sentient beings have *Tathagatagarbha*, they are not separate from the enlightened beings of the Mahayana and Hinayana paths.

What are the differences between the lower path, the middle path (Hinayana or liberation path), and the higher path (Mahayana or Bodhisattva path)? When people practice, they may vow to follow the Bodhisattva path, but they may end up treading the Liberation path, or even the inferior paths of the human and heavenly realms. In the lower paths, a sense of self still exists. It does not matter whether one cultivates precepts, *samadhi*, or wisdom; as long as a self is involved, one will remain on the lower paths. If one practices to become a Buddha, a Bodhisattva, a patriarch, or to become enlightened, then one still clings to a sense of self. These are deluded conceptions of ordinary sentient beings on the lower paths.

The lower path is not bad. It encompasses every level where a sense of self still exists. It can range from the hellish realms to the heavenly realms, from murderers to saints, from people who have never heard the Dharma to people who have achieved a one-mind state. In all cases, there is a self, so it is merely a different level of obscurity. However, although the lower paths are covered by vexation, they are not separate from the lucid, or clear states of the middle and higher paths.

What is the difference between the Bodhisattva path and Liberation path? Some people think that Nirvana begins when one reaches Buddhahood, and then never ends. They also believe that Samsara has existed since beginningless time, but that it ends when one attains Buddhahood. In other words, Samsara has an end, but no beginning, wheras Nirvana has a beginning but no end. These are beliefs of the Liberation, or Hinayana, path.

Such misconceptions are understandable, because Buddhist teachings often describe the path of practice in this manner: one leaves Samsara and enters Nirvana. It seems like Samsara and Nirvana are two separate and distinct places, or conditions. The Bodhisattva, or Mahayana path, teaches that both Samsara and Nirvana are without beginning and end. Samsara and Nirvana are exactly the same thing. "Leaving Samsara and entering Nirvana" is an expedient teaching. Actually, Samsara is Nirvana, wisdom is vexation. In fact, there is no such thing as Nirvana and Samsara, nor wisdom and vexation.

Lucidity, or clarity, refers to complete stillness and complete illumination. In this context, quiescence means

Nirvana. It is a condition where one is not moved by anything. It is complete stillness, utter emptiness. It is the stage described by the empty circle of the *Ten Ox Herding Pictures*. Illumination means wisdom. Only when one's mind is quiescent can wisdom arise. Wisdom manifests as a response to sentient beings. Wisdom has the power to distinguish between vexation and that which is free from vexation. However, it does not manifest for the sake of the enlightened person. It manifests naturally and spontaneously as a response to the needs of the unenlightened. The state of lucidity without wisdom is utter emptiness. If one is completeley still without the aspect of wisdom, then that person cannot function in the world. Such a person has entered Nirvana and is like the great Hinayana arhats.

There paths manifest different levels of clarity, or wisdom. Intellect and logical analysis, however, are not true wisdom. Likewise, any experience or understanding on the lower paths is not true wisdom. People who still travel the lower paths may cultivate supernormal powers, but they are not products of wisdom. If, on the other hand, people on the higher or middle paths achieve supernormal powers, then they are functions of wisdom. In fact, these powers are translated literally from Chinese as "clarities." The sutras speak of three such clarities. The first is called "heavenly eyes," and it refers to the power to see infinitely into the future. The second allows the enlightened person to see infinite past lives. The third is the power of having no more "outflows," or vexations. Only Buddhas have these three clarities.

The wisdom derived from Hinayana practice is a minor clarity. It is not the great wisdom of Mahayana enlightenment. Enlightened practitioners of the Hinayana path clearly perceive a difference between purity and impurity. They distinguish between Samsara and Nirvana. They still make distinctions, even though they are free from greed, hatred and ignorance.

Mahayana practitioners are different. Although the wisdom cultivated from their practice distinguishes between that which is pure and that which is impure, enlightened Mahayana practitioners do not make distinctions for their own sake. They make distinctions in order to help guide ordinary sentint beings on the path to great enlightenment.

> *The four great elements return to their own*
> *nature*
> *As a child finds its mother.*

We know that the four elements are earth, water, fire and wind, but what is meant by nature? Nature here can be understood in two senses. From a philosophical point of view, we can say that every wordly dharma has its own nature, or its own characteristics. For example, water has the characteristic of wetness, fire has the characteristic of warmth, wind has the characteristic of movement, and earth has the characteristic of solidity.

From the point of view of Buddhadharma, nature refers to the self-nature, or original nature, of dharmas. The self-nature of dharmas is empty. In other words, according to Buddhadharma, there is no true self-nature.

From the Madhyamika school of Buddhism comes the following verse: "Because things arise from causes and conditions, it cannot be said that they have genuine existence. Because things arise from causes and conditions, it cannot be said that they have no existence."

From the perspective of ordinary sentient beings, phenomena exist and have their own nature. Buddhadharma says that phenomena (dharmas) have no permanence and arise from causes and conditions. Therefore, they do not have genuine existence. Conventional wisdom says that the four elements exist and are the fundamental basis for all phenomena. Buddhadharma says that even the four elements arise from causes and conditions, and as such, they and the phenomena that arise from them are empty.

The relationship between the four elements and self-nature is as intimate as the relationship between children and their mother. We cannot look at the four elements without regarding their self-nature. Likewise, we cannot look at self-nature without regarding the four elements. A mother is not a mother without children, and children would not exist without a mother.

People without any spiritual or philosophical training only see the superficial manifestations of the interacting four elements. Hence, the minds of ordinary, nonpractitioners are constantly disturbed by phenomena.

People who practice *samadhi,* or who have training in other spiritual or philosophical disciplines, sometimes perceive the world in a more profound way. They clearly see the four elements underlying all phenomena. They can experience a one-mind state – an unmoving mind. People with such awareness will feel that they and all of existence are one. The illusory barrier or discrimination that separates perceiver from perceived is lessened or eliminated altogether. A Confucian saying aptly describes a person with such perception: "If someone suffers, I feel as if I have caused them suffering." This attitude is evident in Christianity. Although it is not Ch'an, it is still a profound and worthwhile experience.

A famous monk named Seng-chao (374-414) wrote a sastra on the *Vimilakirti Sutra.* In his sastras he quoted the sutra as follows: "I see that the *Tathagata* has no beginning and no end. The six entries have been left behind, the three realms have been transcended." This verse describes the Ch'an experience. An enlightened being clearly perceives the four elements, yet he realizes that the four elements do not have genuine existence.

The six entries refer to the eyes, ears, nose, tongue, body and mental consciousness, and the three realms are the same as the five *skandhas.* To transcend the six entries and three realms means that one does not perceive the six senses or the five *skandhas* as having true existence. Realizing that they are empty, however, does not mean that one ignores them or abandons them. Genuinely enlightened beings do not leave Samsara. They remain in the world and help sentient beings. However, they do not have the idea that there are sentient beings to be saved. This is the highest Dharma. It differs from other traditions because enlightened followers of the highest Dharma realize the underlying emptiness of phenomena and the four elements. They see that emptiness, and the phenomena which arise from emptiness, are not separate or different. The *Heart Sutra* says: "Form is not other than emptiness, and emptiness not other than form. Form is precisely emptiness, and emptiness, precisely form."

Enlightened beings sees both the existence and non-existence of phenomena. They see that all phenomena are forever in motion, and at the same time, they see that they are unmoving. Seng-chao wrote the following lines:

> *Great winds are strong enough to tip over*
> > *tall mountains,*
> *But, in fact, nothing changes, nothing*
> > *moves;*
> *All rivers forever run toward the ocean,*
> *Yet, they do not move;*
> *Wild horses run fast, as if they are*
> > *storming the enemy in battle,*
> *But they are not moving;*
> *Sun and moon revolve around the earth,*
> *But actually they never move.*

The motion described in these lines come from the four elements. Enlightened Ch'an practitoners do not deny the movement of the four elements, but in motion they see non-motion – the unmoving state.

A Ch'an saying states, "It is raining on the eastern mountain, yet the western mountain gets wet." This can be understood from two perspectives: the one-mind state and the no-mind state. There is no discrimination in the one-mind state. One sees that the eastern mountain is the same as the western mountain. Therefore, when one mountain is rained upon, the other gets wet. In the no-mind state, or the Ch'an state, the western and eastern mountains have no self-nature. There is no such thing as the western mountain, the eastern mountain, or rain. It makes no difference what is rained upon and what gets wet. On one level, you can say "this is this" and "that is that" – phenomena and the four elements do exist. Essentially, however, they have no genuine existence.

There are three levels of viewing phenomena. The first level includes ordinary sentient beings, who are deluded by phenomena. They do not know and cannot control themselves. They are slaves to the movement of dharmas. The second level includes practitioners who have a better grasp of phenomena. They and phenomena have become one. They make no distinction between subject and object. The third level includes enlightened beings. They have freed themselves from phenomena, yet they do not deny the existence of phenomena.

Actually, there is another level. Hinayana arhats are free from phenomena, but they do not remain in the world. Instead, they enter great emptiness – Nirvana. The Hinayana level is different from the Mahayana experience and Ch'an experience. Thoroughly enlightened people remain in the realm of phenomena, yet they are untouched by phenomena.

Once again, words from Seng-chao to illustrate the ideas of Ch'an: "Although things move (change), they are stationary (unchanging). Although things are stationary, they still move." In other words, although phenomena move and interact, they are fundamentally empty, and unmoving. The second line says that nothing is permanent and enduring. All phenomena incessantly arise and perish.

There is a meditation method called "silent illumination," (silent illumination is not *shikantaza*, the Japanese method of "just sitting.") which is attributed to Hung-chih Cheng-chueh (1091-1157). Silent illumination incorporates both movement and non-movement. Illumination is a process of contemplation, therefore it is moving. Likewise, the object of contemplation is also moving. "Silent" is a quiescent, unmoving state. Only when a people is "silent," or unmoving, can they genuinely observe the true nature of the movement of phenomena. Seng-chao made practical the ideas of movement and stillness by incorporating them into a method. The next lines of the poem are straightforward:

> *Fire burns, wind moves and shakes,*
> *Water moistens, earth solidifies.*
> *Eyes – forms, ears – sounds,*
> *Nose – odors, tongue – salt and sour.*

The first couplet refers to the four elements, and the second couplet refers to the six sense organs and their six sense objects. Taken together, Shih-t'ou is referring to all phenomena: the four elements, the five *skandhas*, and the eighteen realms (the six sense organs, the six sense objects, and the six sense consciousnesses).

The two couplets talk about self-nature in the worldly sense, describing characteristics of the four elements and the sense organs. These are all worldly characteristics or functions of dharmas. But, from the Ch'an perspective, all of these things are illusory and transitory, because they arise from causes and conditions. They have no genuine self-nature. They have no genuine existence.

> *In accordance with each dharma,*
> *The root gives rise to separate leaves.*
> *Roots and branches must return to basic*
> *   principle;*
> *"Honorable" and "lowly" are merely words.*

Each of the four elements, six senses and six sense objects has its unique functions and characteristics. These are represented by the leaves in the verses above. What are the roots? As I said earlier, there are two kinds of nature. First is the unique nature of all dharmas. This nature is temporary and changes with causes and conditions. Second is the self-nature, or foundation, of all dharmas. It is unmoving. Every dharma arises and perishes according to its causes and conditions, but like a tree, the many leaves come from the same root. The root is the foundation of all dharmas. The root is unmoving.

The first couplet says that out of emptiness comes existence. The leaves are the dharmas that are influenced by causes and conditions. The roots are emptiness, from which dharmas arise. Existence comes out of emptiness. Through existence we can perceive emptiness.

The next line reverses the direction of the first idea. It says from emptiness we can perceive the changing dharmas that arise from causes and conditions. Which realization occurs during meditation? Does one see emptiness in existence? Or does one see existence rising from emptiness? Does one first realize emptiness, and then look out and perceive phenomena? Or, in looking at phenomena, does one perceive emptiness. Emphasizing only the second way, that of existence rising from emptiness, is the view of Hinayana *pratekyabuddhas*, who permanently enter Nirvana because they perceive all phenomena as being unreal.

Actually, root and leaves are one. In order to talk about them we use these terms: ultimate truth and worldly truth – or, in the case of this translation, honorable and lowly. These two terms are one and the same. They are merely words used to help explain concepts. This is the actual meaning of the line, "Roots and branches must return to the basic principle."

The ultimate truth and worldly truth are one, yet they mutually interact. It is the same with brightness and darkness. One cannot exist without the other. Without brightness, there is no such thing as darkness. There can be two, but never one. It is the same with the analogy of leaves and roots. The highest Buddhadharma transcends all discriminations.

Mahayana looks at Hinayana and considers it inferior, but Ch'an looks at Mahayana and Hinayana as the same. The leaves are not separate from root and root is not separate from leaves.

In another analogy, wife and husband cannot exist without the other. They establish one another. There can be no wife without a husband and no husband without a wife. It is the same with existence and emptiness. Existence can be established only in relation to emptiness. Emptiness can be established only because of existence. Emptiness belongs to existence. Existence belongs to emptiness. They form a mutually interacting duality.

Do you see existence and then see emptiness? Or do you see emptiness and then existence? There is a difference. When you are practicing, there is something you must experience first. When you experience enlightenment, which nature do you see into?

Ordinarily, when people initially experience enlightenment, the first thing they see into is emptiness. This is not ultimate enlightenment, but it is a beginning. In Theravadan Buddhism, you realize emptiness by analyzing phenomena. This kind of emptiness is called analytical emptiness, but it is not the experience of Ch'an.

In Ch'an enlightenment, you realize that existence is not different from emptiness. Simultaneously, there is neither emptiness nor existence. If you only see emptiness, then this is an "outer path" experience. In a Ch'an experience, phenomena are still there. You see and interact with phenomena, but in your mind they are empty. They are empty, yet they are right there at that moment.

The concepts above are part of the Madhyamika school of Buddhism. Madhyamika is considered the highest philosophical teaching – but it is mainly contemplation. Madhyamika reasons, Ch'an experiences. Madhyamika provides direct contemplation for those whose views are beset with obstacles. A practitioner of the Madhyamika school, through reasoning, can directly experience wisdom, but the level of experience is not as deep as that which can be experienced through Ch'an methods. Ch'an does away with contemplation and directly practices and experiences. However, Madhyamika methods can also bring liberation. In fact, only those who have had deep enlightenments experiences can clearly understand and speak Madhyamika philosophy.

> *In the midst of brightness there is*
> > *darkness;*
> *Do not take darkness as darkness.*
> *In the midst of darkness there is*
> > *brightness;*
> *Do not take brightness as brightness.*

These couplets are straightforward. In darkness there is brightness, and in brightness there is darkness. They exist in one another. It is easy to understand, but in our actual experiences there is no such thing. If you extinguish all lights in a room, there is only darkness. If you turn on the lights, there is only brightness.

Answer this: Before you were born did you have the same body? Every second you are changing. You are not the same as you were even a minute ago. Obviously your body was different before you were born. Taken to its logical conclusion, you would probably admit that there is no such thing as "your" body. You will discover the same is true for your mind. Therefore, there is no such thing as "you." But if you accept and cling to this concept alone, it is an "outer path" understanding. It is a harsh misconception not to acknowledge the self, to see only emptiness.

If brightness were separate from darkness, when I turn on the lights, darkness would vanish. There would be no such thing as darkness anymore. It would always be bright. In darkness there is brightness. When I turn on the light, darkness is still there. In essence, brightness and darkness are one and the same. They cannot be separated. If I tell someone to leave the room, it does not mean that person does not exist anymore.

Things exist in contrast to other things. Things exist because we discriminate. People separate vexation from wisdom. They try to avoid vexation and attain wisdom. In fact, vexation and wisdom exist only in our minds because we contrast them. One exists because of the other. Ultimately, they are one and the same thing. A passage in the *Platform Sutra* says: "Life and death are themselves Nirvana. Vexation is itself wisdom." These are Mahayana concepts. These words are not Ch'an Dharma, because they still make distinctions. The ultimate truth is that there is no life, death, or Nirvana. Nirvana and Samsara, vexation and wisdom, are all one. In truth, there is nothing to talk about.

> *Brightness and darkness correspond,*
> *Like one step following another.*

Brightness and darkness correspond to one another, but it does not mean that they are in fixed contrast to one another. Rather, they mutually interact. When we walk, our legs must work together. One leg has to follow the other. When one is forward, the other must be behind, and to walk, both legs must keep moving back and forth. They cannot be fixed in one position. You cannot separate Nirvana from Samsara and wisdom from vexation. Ch'an is in the world and also apart from the world. It is apart from the world, but not away from it.

I am using worldly examples to explain ultimate truth. Ultimately, nothing I say can express the real meaning. You cannot compare worldly Dharma with Ch'an Dharma. You cannot explain ultimate principles. You must experience them.

Hinayana practitioners strive to leave Samsara and enter Nirvana. Enlightened Mahayana practitioners, though they have realized Nirvana, still abide in Samsara to help others. They do not abandon Samsara. The highest teaching is different. It says that birth and death are one. There is no such thing as separating birth and death from Nirvana, or vexation from wisdom.

If vexation and wisdom are one, does it mean we do

not have to practice? Listening to words and pondering concepts are not true experiences. To truly know that vexation and wisdom are one, you must practice. You must experience it directly.

> *All things have their own function*
> *Depending on their use and location.*

This couplet speaks of phenomena from the viewpoint of differentiation. There are two kinds of differentiation. First is differentiation with attachment. It is illusory differentiation – a vexation. Second is differentiation that manifests from wisdom. Differentiation that arises from wisdom is used to help sentient beings. Buddhism sometimes speaks of the great functions of the three kinds of karma – that of body, speech and mind. An enlightened person uses the faculties of body, speech and mind to deliver sentient beings.

Fully enlightened beings do not discriminate as do ordinary sentient beings. They do not make distinctions with minds of attachment, and they do not view the world dualistically. Ordinary sentient beings think that liberated beings act and discriminate like normal people. In fact, the interaction of enlightened beings and unenlightened beings is itself differentiation. However, completely enlightened beings do not attach to phenomena. They respond to phenomena, but not with a mind of attachment. Such people look normal to us. They eat, sleep, walk, talk, work and laugh, yet the source of their actions, thoughts and words are wisdom, not attachment. They react to phenomena spontaneously, immediately, and without intellectual discrimination. Their actions stem from an immediate intuition whose source is wisdom, and they respond to the needs of sentient beings as a result of their vows. Thoroughly enlightened beings are not blocks of wood or zombies. They are fully aware and fully functioning.

As I said earlier, each dharma has two self-natures. One is self-nature that is common to all things. It is emptiness. The other is the specific characteristic of each individual dharma. It is illusory self-nature. Enlightened people see emptiness. They perceive that every dharma is the same and that there are no distinctions. Enlightened beings are also aware of specific dharmas, or illusory dharmas. They recognize that each dharma has its characteristics. They are not idiots. They know the difference between fire and water; but, illusory dharmas do not interfere or move enlightened beings. Enlightened beings are not phased by phenomena, yet they interact with phenomena. If you ask an enlightened master his name, he will answer you. In that sense, he is no different from you. Fire will burn his body, but it has nothing to do with his true nature.

> *Phenomena stores, seals, covers, combines.*
> *Principle yields to the arrow, the sword's*
>   *edge, the stick.*

Phenomena are not separate from principle, and principle is not separate from phenomena. Phenomena contains the principle. Principle is never separate from phenomena. The first line says that within phenomena exists that which is sealed, covered, and combined, all of which refer to principle. The sword, stick, and arrow of the second line refer to phenomena – that which is on the surface, that which arises from emptiness.

Phenomena contains within it the principle. Within sentient beings, the principle is sometimes called *Tathagatagarbha*. All worldy dharmas contain within them the self-nature of emptiness.

Unenlightened people are not aware of the principle. After an initial enlightenment, practitioners usually perceive that the principle, or emptiness, is separate from phenomena. They view emptiness as an entity in itself. This is erroneous.

If it were the case that principle and phenomena were separate, then sentient beings would eternally remain sentient beings. They would never attain Buddhahood. Buddhahood would be unreachable.

Some schools of Buddhism believe that there are sentient beings who will never reach Buddhahood. Mahayana Buddhism disagrees. All sentient beings are potential Buddhas. Everything contains Buddha-nature. If rocks and clouds have Buddha-nature, then all sentient beings must have Buddha-nature as well.

If someone does not believe in Buddha, does it mean that that person does not have Buddha-nature? No. Not only do all sentient beings have Buddha-nature, all people are Bodhisattvas. This is so because a person's position, attitude, actions and beliefs are temporary. In this lifetime he may not follow Buddhadharma, but he still has the potential to attain Buddhahood. Eventually he will follow the Bodhisattva path. Therefore, all people are Bodhisattvas.

Many believe that there are good people and bad people, but eventually all people will return to their true nature. Similarly, phenomena are never apart from emptiness, no matter how illusory they are. Without phenomena, emptiness cannot exist. Emptiness can only be seen within phenomena. Apart from phenomena, there is no way one could recognize emptiness.

> *Received teachings must be reconciled with*
> *basic principle;*
> *Do not establish your own rules.*

No matter what you read, what you learn, no matter how Buddhadharma is explained, all of it is expedient teaching. I might speak of enlightenment and practice, but it is separate from the fundamental principle. As long as we speak and use our minds, we must remain aware that we are discriminating. The fundamental principle is non-differentiation. Whatever can be described is only an expedient teaching.

Buddhadharma exists for those who are unenlightened. The Tao exists for people who are still walking the Buddha path. Those who are fully enlightened understand that the Tao is not the true path. It is a convenient teaching for those who need to be taught.

When a bird flies across the sky, it doesn't leave a

trace. There was no trace before the bird arrived, and there will be no trace after the bird departs. Still, we speak of the bird's path. The Dharma spoken by Buddha and the path transmitted by the Patriarchs are like traces left behind by birds. If you say there is such a thing as the Buddha path, that would be incorrect. However, if you say there is no such thing as the Buddha path, that would also be incorrect.

We should not be attached to the words of the Buddha. Buddha never said that he had spoken the ultimate truth. In fact, he said he spoke not a word in his forty-nine years of teaching. His teachings were only expedient methods. He also said that his words were medicine for a given sickness at a given time.

> *Using your eyes, the path is lost.*
> *Using your feet, how can you know the road?*

The principle and phenomena are not polar opposites. They mutually interact. If you rely on your eyes, then you do not understand the principle that is behind phenomena. If you rely on your senses and differentiating mind, then you will never see the underlying emptiness of all dharmas.

If you rely only on your feet, you will not know where you are going. In other words, if you practice without a proper understanding of Buddhadharma, then you will get lost on the outer paths. Many people practice in order to attain goals. I always tell practitioners that the goal of practice is practice. There is no other goal. Practice itself is the path. If, in your practice, you have no goals, no expectations, no attachments, then principle and phenomena are in accordance with one another.

> *Moving forward there is no near or far;*
> *Confusion creates mountains and rivers of*
> *obstructions.*

Usually, when people first begin to practice, they ask me how long it will take to attain enlightenment or derive benefit from their efforts. They think that attending retreats and sitting in groups will shorten their journey. It is not true.

The beginning is the end. If you are confused, then you are at the beginning. If you experience enlightenment, then you are instantly at the end. When vexations return, you are at the beginning again. For example, Hui-neng was enlightened before he ever met the Fifth Patriarch. He was at the end before he ever started formal practice.

After Hui-neng received the robe and bowl and became the Sixth Patriarch, he had to escape from jealous rivals. One monk, Hui-ming, caught up with him and asked for his teaching. At that moment the monk had a discriminating mind. He was a beginner. Hui-neng asked him, "Thinking neither of good nor evil, what is your original nature?" Upon hearing his words, Hui-ming immediately got enlightened. At that moment, he was at the end.

If you "understand" right in this moment, then you

are already at the end. Practitioners should not be disappointed or anxious. Such thoughts and feelings create obstructions the size of great mountains and wide rivers. If, however, you seek nothing, and you possess neither love nor hate, then you will be enlightened instantly.

Those who practice Ch'an in the correct manner do so for the sake of practice. People ask me, "If practice is its own goal, what do you do after you finish practicing?" There is no end to practice. Buddha, who had infinite wisdom and merit, taught sentient beings. That was his practice.

There should be no goals in your practice. You should not think, "I want to get enlightened. After that, I'll be satisfied." If you think such thoughts, you are far from the path and enlightenment. Thinking in such manner creates insurmountable mountains and uncrossable rivers on the path. If you have no goals, and just practice, that moment is liberation.

There is a saying "If for a single thought you are in accordance with the Dharma, then for that moment you are like the Buddha. If you remain in accordance thought after thought, then you remain the same as the Buddha. If, in a single thought, attachment arises, then you are away from Buddha."

The last couplet reads:

> *I implore those who investigate the*
> *   mysterious:*
> *Do not waste your time!*

Shih-t'ou sincerely implores practitioners not to waste time. When you have attachments or have a mind of gain and loss, then you cannot understand that wisdom and vexation are the same. Life is short, and Buddhadharma precious, so practice hard. Use every waking moment, whether it is spent in meditation or in daily activities, to practice. Turn your everyday life into practice. Anything else is a waste of time.

THE SONG OF THE PRECIOUS MIRROR SAMADHI

by Tung-shan Liang-chieh (807-869)

It is this very Dharma
The Buddha and Patriarchs secretly transmitted.
Now that you have it
Protect it well.

Like a silver bowl full of snow
Or an egret hidden against the bright moon
They are similar but not identical.
When mingled their difference can be recognized.

The meaning does not lie in words,
Yet those who are ripe must be taught.
As soon as you act it is a dead issue,
So consider their varying attainments.

Rejecting words or clinging to them are both mistakes,
Like a blazing fire, useful but dangerous.
If it is only expressed in language
The precious mirror will be stained.

At midnight it is truly bright;
By daylight it no longer shows.
It serves as the law which governs all things;
Use it to uproot all suffering.
Though it is not a way of action

Still, it is not without words.
As before the precious mirror,
The form and reflection gaze on each other.
You are not it,
But it is just you.

Just as an infant
Is equipped with five sense organs.
It neither comes nor goes,
It neither arises nor abides.

P'o-p'o H'o-h'o –
A phrase without meaning.
You can never get the substance of it
Because the language is not correct.

Doubling the Li trigram makes six lines.
The outer and inner lines mutually interact.
Stacked, they become three pairs;
At most they can transform into five.

Like the five aromas of the hyssop plant
Or the five branches of the vajra scepter.
The exact center subtly harmonizing,
Drumming and singing simultaneously.

Penetrate the goal and you will fathom the way.
In order to lead there must be a road.
To be wrong is auspicious;
Do not oppose it.
Natural and subtle
It is neither ignorance nor enlightenment
Causes and conditions have their time and season,
Tranquil and illuminating.

It is so small it enters the spaceless,
So large it is beyond dimension.
If you are off by a hair's breadth
Then you would be out of harmony.

Now there is sudden and gradual (enlightenment)
In order to establish the fundamental guidelines.
When the fundamental guidelines are clear
They become the rule.

Realization of the basic principle is the ultimate
        standard,
Genuine, constant, yet flowing,
With still body but racing mind,
Like a tethered horse or a mouse frozen by fright.

Past sages pitied them
And liberated them with Buddhadharma.
Following their upside-down ways
They took black for white.
When inverted thinking disappears,
They realize mind of their own accord.

If you want to merge with the ancient track
Then contemplate the ancients.
At the completion of the Buddha path
Ten kalpas of contemplation will be established.

Like a tiger's lame foot,
Like a shoeless horse,
Because there is a defect
You seek the jeweled bench and priceless halter.
Because you are astonished
You realize you were like the brown or white ox.

Hou-i used his skill
To hit the target at a hundred paces.
As soon as the arrow hits the mark
Of what further use is his skill?

When a wooden man breaks into song,
A stone woman gets up to dance.
Since this cannot be understood by reasoning
How can it be analyzed?

The minister serves his lord;
The son obeys his father.
If he does not obey, he is not filial;
If the minister does not serve, he is not loyal.

To cultivate in hiding, functioning in secret,
Like a fool, like a dolt;
If only you are able to persist,
You will be called a master among masters.

Introduction

The *Song of the Precious Mirror Samadhi* was written by Tung-shan Liang-chieh, a master of the Ts'ao-tung sect of Ch'an Buddhism. I will not discuss the life and experiences of this enlightened master. Instead, I will concentrate on the song itself. Before I comment on the verses, however, I wish to give an overview of the song, and place it in its proper historical Buddhist context.

The *Song of the Precious Mirror Samadhi* belongs to the Ts'ao-tung sect of Ch'an Buddhism. The Rinzai sect and Soto sect of Zen Buddhism are derived from the Lin-chi sect and Ts'ao-tung sect of Ch'an Buddhism. Although the Chinese Ch'an sects and the Japanese Zen sects are in large part similar, one should not presume that they are exactly the same. The founder of the Soto sect, Dogen Zenji (1200-1253) and the founder of the Rinzai sect, Myoan Eisai (1141-1215) introduced the Ts'ao-tung and Lin-chi schools teachings to Japan during the thirteenth century. In the ensuing centuries, the Soto and Rinzai schools have evolved through the influence of Japanese history and culture. In this commentary, I will speak mainly on the Ts'ao-tung sect's teachings; therefore, omission of other teachings is inevitable. In no way do I wish to denigrate or de-emphasize the importance of other schools of Buddhism.

The Ts'ao-tung sect, while it is a "sudden enlightenment" school, places heavy emphasis on philosophy. A reference is made in the first chapter of *The Principle of the Five Sects* (written in 1857 by an unknown author), comparing the Ts'ao-tung sect with the Lin-chi sect. It says that if one practices only Lin-chi methods, yet knows nothing of the Ts'ao-tung sect, then that person will be like "wild fox" Ch'an practitioners.

Similarly, if one practices the Ts'ao-tung methods, but has no understanding of the Lin-chi sect, then that person will be lost in a web of teachings; lost in words and language. Therefore, in order to succeed in Ch'an practice, one must understand the Lin-chi and Ts'ao-tung sects together. If one masters these two sects, then one will automatically understand the other three sects: Wei-yang, Yun-men, and Fa-yen. The fact that it can be perilous to follow either school too intensely does not mean that one must study and follow the teachings of both the Lin-chi and Ts'ao-tung schools. Rather, it is a way of pointing out the differences between the two schools' approaches to practice.

Wild fox Ch'an refers to people who read a few kung-ans with no real understanding and then claim that scriptures are not necessary, and that one need not listen to the teachings or even use methods of practice. They claim that Ch'an is before any of this, and they believe that without relying on Buddhadharma, they have already entered Ch'an. People with these deluded ideas say things similar to the teachings of the great patriarchs, but they do not have true understanding, and their words are empty.

At the other extreme, followers of the philosophy-laden Ts'ao-tung sect, who have not penetrated the teachings, are entangled in words and ideas.

Most Mahayana Buddhist sects borrow terminology from other schools of thought (Indian traditions, Taoism, Confucianism, etc.) to explain the concepts and levels of practice of Ch'an. This is especially true of the Ts'ao-tung school. For instance, in the *Song of the Precious Mirror Samadhi*, ideas are borrowed from the *I Ching*.

The teachings of the Ts'ao-tung sect are difficult to penetrate because one needs to have an understanding of many other spiritual and philosphical traditions. For those who are not familiar with the concepts of other traditions, Ts'ao-tung teachings are impenetrable. There is also a danger that words taken out of the proper context will be misconstrued. Even those people who are familiar with Taoism, Confucianism, or the *I Ching*, have to be careful. They must also understand fundamental concepts of Ch'an. If practitioners are not in accord with Ch'an teachings, they will understand the Taoist or Confucianist meaning, and take it to be Ch'an. For these reasons, one must take care in studying Ts'ao-tung teachings.

The title, *Song of the Precious Mirror Samadhi*, deserves special attention. Why does Tung-shan speak of a precious mirror? The mirror is often used as a symbol in Buddhist teachings. The sutras speak of an ancient mirror; so old, it is completely covered with dust; so ancient, people have forgotten that they possess the precious mirror.

A *kung-an* tells of a master and a disciple traveling through the mountains. They see a group of monkeys, and the master comments that the creatures are truly pitiable, for though they carry the ancient mirror, they run around in confusion and ignorance.

The symbol of the mirror also appears in a story in the *Surangama Sutra*: A woman wakes up one morning, looks in the mirror and sees her reflection. She is afraid, because she doesn't recognize the person in the mirror. After a moment, she realizes, "That's my head!" She rubs her eyes and takes another look, but her reflection is gone again. Desperate, she searches frantically for her head.

The two stories are different, yet they both use the mirror as a symbol. In the story of the woman and her reflection, the mirror is outside of her self. She has forgotten that her head is on her shoulders; she thinks it is in the mirror. In essence, she has forgotten her self. In the story of the monkeys, the mirror refers to our true selves. Though we have never seen this mirror, it is there. The mirror symbol in the *Song of the Precious Mirror Samadhi* is closer in meaning to the story of the monkeys. The mirror is our true self. It is precious because no matter how long it has been hidden, forgotten, and covered with dust, it never loses its power of illumination and reflection.

The precious mirror is not an ordinary mirror, so the analogy must be stretched. An ordinary mirror has a finite shape and size. It has sides, a front and a back. The precious mirror, however, has no boundaries. It cannot be defined in terms of shape and size.

Some early Buddhist masters also used the circle as a symbol of true nature. Recorded incidences often depict disciples asking masters what the Buddha is like, or what self-nature is, or what the essence of the Buddha's teachings is. In one case, a master formed a circle with his fingers, and then made a motion of throwing it away. In another case, a different master traced a circle on the ground with a stick, and then erased the circle. The circle represents something that is perfect, but it is only a finite symbol. For this reason, the masters disposed of the circles. One must not form attachments to teachings and confuse symbols with reality. Circles and mirrors are merely symbols of true nature. After they are used to make a point, they must be discarded.

The precious mirror is a symbol of the foundation of all dharmas, the source of all sentient beings, the substance of all Buddhas. Many other names and terms referring to the same thing exist. At different times I may refer to it as self-nature, pure nature, or original nature.

In the *Avatamsaka Sutra*, it is called the One True Dharma Realm. In the *Lotus Sutra*, it is called the One True Nature. In the *Nirvana Sutra*, it is called the Great Nirvana, the Secret Store, or Buddha-nature. In the *Surangama Sutra*, it is called the Tathagatagarbha (Tathagata Store). The Consciousness Only school refers to it as the Alaya Consciousness or the Great Perfect Mirror Wisdom. In the end, however, it is best to remember that they are only names.

From what we know of the meaning of "precious mirror," it would seem that "Song of the Precious Mirror" would suffice as a title, yet Tung-shan calls his poem the *Song of the Precious Mirror Samadhi. Samadhi*, like "precious mirror," has special meaning in the context of Tung-shan's title. *Samadhi* refers to the power of the precious mirror, which manifests only when one attains the most profound level of *samadhi.* At this stage, all attachments fall away. The power that manifests is twofold: it benefits oneself by removing vexations, and it benefits others by helping them find their own precious mirror. This is the power – the *samadhi* – of the precious mirror.

Song of the Precious Mirror Samadhi

Several Buddhist works have been written in the form of songs or poems. Perhaps the most famous is the *Song of Enlightenment*. A teaching written in verse is easily communicated to others. Verse helps the reader absorb material quickly and thoroughly.

In the Ts'ao-tung sect, the *Song of the Precious Mirror Samadhi* was used to transmit the Dharma from master to disciple. People who wanted to follow the teachings and practice the methods of the Ts'ao-tung sect were given this song to study and memorize.

Now we will enter the song. The first two lines:

> *It is this very Dharma*
> *The Buddha and Patriarchs secretly*
> *transmitted.*

The first two lines state that the Dharma is transmitted in private. It is not a public announcement. It is similar to two people having a code that they and only they understand. The first historic transmission occurred between Sakyamuni Buddha and his disciple, Mahakasyapa. After giving a sermon to his senior disciples, Sakyamuni Buddha picked up a flower and held it silently before the assembly. All the monks except one were mystified. Mahaskayapa alone understood the Buddha's meaning, and he smiled in response. Thus, Sakyamuni transmitted the Dharma to Mahakasyapa, the first patriarch. In turn, Mahakasyapa transmitted the Dharma to his successor, and so on, generation after generation to the present.

The Dharma that is transmitted is precisely this precious mirror *samadhi*–true nature. It is secret in that it is known only by enlightened Buddhists, patriarchs and masters. Only the master and the disciple to whom it is being transmitted are aware of it. Those who do not fully understand the Dharma have no idea of what is happening. Sakyamuni lifts a flower, Mahaskayapa smiles, and the Dharma is transmitted. No one else understands.

According to the sutras, however, Budddha-dharma is innate in all sentient beings. It does not have to be given to us by the Buddha. It does not have to be passed from master to disciple. The Ch'an sect maintains that nothing is transmitted. Dharma is within us, so there is no need for transmission. What, then, is the transmission referred to in the first two lines of the *Song of the Precious Mirror Samadhi?* It is true that there is a formal ritual, where something is given or transmitted, but it is only a ritual. Nothing is really given by a master to his disciple. The ritual is simply an affirmation that the master and disciple have come to the same understanding. The master is giving his seal of approval.

An analogy would be the diploma a student receives upon graduation. It represents the student's education; it affirms that the student has attended school for a certain period of time and has passed the examinations. But the diploma has no intrinsic value. It is not knowledge. It is a symbol. During the T'ang dynasty, a scholar wrote an article about teachers and masters, which said that their functions are to transmit the path or the truth, to teach the students the proper course of work and study, and finally, to help students in their removal of doubt. Later, during the Ming dynasty, Master Ou-i, a Buddhist monk, commented on the article. He said that a teacher does indeed possess the latter two functions, that of teaching a proper course and removing doubt, but one person does not transmit the Buddha path to another person. The path exists everywhere: in ashes, in clay, in hair.

Where, then, is this path, this Tao? Is it in clay pots and fireplaces? Is it in your hair? Does it mean the path shrinks when you get a haircut? What about me, I'm bald? If you went beyond hair and cut off your head, would you succeed in removing the Tao? No, this is all foolishness. Cutting off your head is nothing more than suicide. It does, however, raise an interesting question. Can killing be the Tao? If we understand it as a way of doing something, or getting somewhere, then killing cannot be considered a path. But if we understand the Tao as the ultimate reality, then in that sense there is no such thing as killing or not killing.

Where there is a conception of good and evil, right and wrong, there is still attachment. If you consider killing to be evil, and helping good, then you are still relying on the concepts of ordinary sentient beings. A truly liberated being has no attachments to conceptions of good and evil.

The precious mirror is unlimited. It is Buddha-nature, true reality. It can have form; it can be formless. Form and non-form, sentient beings and non-sentient beings, all have the same perfect nature as the Buddha, the same perfect wisdom as the Buddha.

> *Now that you have it*
> *Protect it well.*

These two lines are advice from master to disciple. A glimpse of the precious mirror is not Buddhahood. A disciple might have an experience of enlightenment, but it is not ultimate enlightenment. Enlightenment disappears when vexations arise. Therefore, when the master acknowledges a disciple's understanding, he also gives a warning. There is gain and loss with this experience. What the disciple has gained is the understanding or the vision of the precious mirror. The master has affirmed a level of understanding. However, if this understanding is not protected through diligent practice, it will be lost again. This is generally called, "sudden enlightenment, gradual cultivation."

A clean mirror reflects perfectly. A mirror covered with dust or steam no longer reflects. One would like to keep one's mirror clean forever, but it is not always possible. The same applies to Buddha-nature. If you see your precious mirror, protect it well, or it will be covered with the dust and steam of vexation again. Do not despair, however, if, having momentarily glimpsed your self-nature, you watch it disappear under layers of vexation. Finding the mirror and then losing it is not as bad as never having seen it. Seeing the precious mirror increases your faith that it exists, and you will continue practicing with even greater determination.

One might think that Buddha-nature is not worth much if it can be found and then lost again. It is true that something genuine cannot be gained or lost. If something is truly real, then it must be permanent, indestructible. Hair that can be cut is not genuine; a body that ages and dies is not truly real. But enlightenment is different. "I'm enlightened" and "I'm no longer enlightened" are just expressions. Enlightenment is not gained or lost. When someone becomes enlightened, it is Buddha-nature manifested. And when enlightenment is lost, it is Buddha-nature covered by vexation. Whether the mirror is clear or covered, the mirror is still there. Just so with Buddha-nature. It is the reflecting power that is gained or lost.

How can one protect this enlightened state after it is reached? There are two ways. The first is to use great energy, and practice intensely until one attains great enlightenment. It is like burning weeds in a field. An ordinary fire will scorch the ground, but the roots of the weeds remain, and they will sprout again. An intense fire, however, will burn even the deepest roots, and nothing will grow in that field again. This is great practice. A perfect description can be found in the *Platform Sutra*. Before he became the Sixth Patriarch, Hui-neng wrote four lines of verse describing ultimate enlightenment. It was in response to another monk's (Shen-hsiu) description of enlightenment:

> *There is no Bodhi-tree,*
> *Nor stand of a mirror bright.*
> *Since all is void,*
> *Where can the dust alight?*

The second way, described in the verse written by Shen-hsiu (606?-706), is to protect the mirror mind by constantly wiping it clean of dust, of vexation. Before reaching the level of "no mirror," one must strive to clean the precious mirror. If one is relentlessly diligent, the enlightened state can be protected. This requires ceaseless practice.

Someone once told me that in her practice she saw her vexations, but she did not have the discipline to continually wipe them away. She said she would wait until she was in a better state of mind. I told her that she had the wrong attitude. If you see dust or stains on a mirror, it would be best to wipe them off as soon as you notice them, and not wait for more and more to collect. Of course I am talking about the mind and not a mirror. Cleaning a mirror is easy, but perhaps not so the mind. How is it accomplished? The very act of recognizing the dust, or vexations, on your mirror mind cleans the dust away. No other method is necessary.

There is a difference between the two methods described by Hui-neng and Shen-hsiu. The second method requires continual practice. The first method requires an energy so powerful that no practice is necessary after great enlightenment is attained. At that point, the analogy of the mirror no longer applies. Such attainment is rare.

There is a third way, but it is not part of the proper Ch'an practice. The methods people tried reached an extreme during Sakyamuni Buddha's lifetime. Monks who had attained arhatship thought that they had completely dropped their egos and reached the final state of enlightenment. Afraid that it would not be permanent, they committed suicide. This practice was banned by the Buddha.

In a more moderate variation of this method, some monks and nuns leave society and live in solitude for the rest of their lives in the hope that they will avoid vexation. Practicing in solitude is a recommended form of practice, but at some point it is necessary to rejoin society. The extreme approach of these left-home practitioners is incorrect. Living in solitude, you will experience less vexation, but you may be mislead into thinking that you have accomplished more than you really have. It is like lighting a candle in the dark, and then covering it with a blanket because you fear that the wind will blow out the flame. The flame exists, but it is feeble and of little use.

Ch'an methods direct you to train your mind wherever you are – alone, with people, on Times Square. Clean the mirror, and forget the environment. I spent six years alone in the mountains, but my vexations did not disappear, and when I returned, they did not greatly increase. The vexations were more a product of my mind than of the environment I lived in.

Although it is recommended that serious practitioners spend time in practice away from society, one should not completely abandon humanity. You cannot run away from the world. I may have many vexations, but I also have compassion. I am not an arhat. I am only an ordinary sentient being. Sometimes I see my vexations coming down like snow flakes in a winter storm, dropping on my mirror. But through constant practice, I keep my mirror warm, and the snow quickly melts away.

> *Like a silver bowl full of snow*
> *Or an egret hidden against the bright moon*
> *They are similar but not identical.*
> *When mingled their difference can be*
>   *recognized.*

These four lines describe how the enlightened person sees the world. Ordinarily, we think that the mind of an enlightened person is unmoving. However, it cannot be said that there is no thought in his mind. There are thoughts, but the way that thoughts arise and perish in the enlightened mind is different from the way they rise and fall in the ordinary mind. If an enlightened mind literally does not move, then one could argue that an enlightened being is no different from a block of wood, a stone, or a dead person. It is true that enlightenment is a "no-mind" state, but it is not the same as the state of a rock or corpse. The mind of an enlightened person still functions. The enlightened mind also differs from an ordinary mind, but only the enlightened being understands and detects the difference.

The first two lines of the stanza contain analogies, which describe things similar but not the same. The silver bowl and bright moon are unmoving. They represent the enlightened mind. They signify wisdom. The snow, which is placed in the bowl, is something moving, in the sense that it is transitory. By containing the snow (the object), the bowl (the subject) manifests a function – namely, to contain something. In a similar sense, the moon illuminates the egret. The snow and egret symbolize phenomena of the external environment and the mental realm (thoughts) as well. What ordinary people view as thoughts, enlightened beings see as objects of the mental realm. As such, they are no longer thoughts in the ordinary sense. An enlightened person can use thoughts expediently to help a sentient being. Thoughts are tools for an enlightened person; they are functions of wisdom. To a fully enlightened person, vexation is no different from wisdom, and so vexation can be used as a means of helping others.

In the first line, there is the subject/silver bowl, and the object/snow. In the second line there is the subject/bright moon and the object/egret. The snow and the bowl are the same color, but they are not the same things. The same is true for the egret and the moon.

Enlightened beings see everything as one, but they

can make distinctions; that is why they can see that the snow is not the bowl, the egret not the moon. But ordinary beings see everything as separate. For unenlightened people, there are only distinctions. If this stanza were written from an ordinary being's point of view, the object and subject would be very different. Instead of a white bird, there would be a crow flying past the moon; instead of snow, something brightly colored would be placed in a silver bowl. Ordinary people make very clear distinctions between themselves and what they are observing, and between one object and another. An enlightened person, however, makes no such distinctions between "you and I," "this and that."

Does an enlightened being perceive a father and a son to be the same? Does an enlightened being see both as fathers, both as sons? To an enlightened being, everything is the same. The external realm and the mental realm are one and the same. Nonetheless, the enlightened person still sees the distinctions that ordinary people see.

An enlightened being can function as an ordinary person. In fact, an ordinary person would see nothing unusual about an enlightened being. But an enlightened being is different. He makes no distinctions between near and far, good and bad.

After attaining Buddhahood, Sakyamuni still recognized his father as his father, his wife as his wife. When his father died, Sakyamuni participated in the funeral service as would be expected of any son. Though he did not perceive a father-son relationship in the same way an ordinary person would, he followed worldly convention, and fulfilled his responsibility as a son.

> *The meaning does not lie in words,*
> *Yet those who are ripe must be taught.*
> *As soon as you act it is a dead issue,*
> *So consider their varying attainments.*

This stanza explains the actions of an enlightened master. A master does not teach in any specific form, with any specific words or methods. He will help someone with the right causes and conditions in any way he can. There is no fixed method or instruction.

Once the master acts – offers instruction, gives a method, presents a *kung-an* – the act is dead. Acts occur in response to causes and conditions, and are never apart from causes and conditions. Since causes and conditions are always changing, the acts that respond to them are always changing. Once an act transpires, that same act never transpires again, because the causes and conditions will never be the same. This means that the master cannot repeat the same approach again with a different person, or even with the same person at different times. Just as different prescriptions are needed for different illnesses, so too are different instructions needed for different students.

As the last line states, a master must "consider the varying attainments" of each disciple. When I teach someone, I carefully consider that person's background, personality, nature and manner, and then use the appropriate method, the method that I feel is best suited for this individual.

This stanza provides a model for how a master should interact with a disciple. The first line is a common Buddhist phrase: "The meaning does not lie in words." Although the ultimate principle cannot be expressed in words, an enlightened person still uses words to help others. But words are always different because the situations are always different.

In Buddhadharma there is a four-part saying: "Rely on the Dharma, not the person; Rely on the principle, not the word; Rely on wisdom, not the discriminating mind; Rely on ultimate principle, not the mundane." This saying expresses ultimate principles, and with these principles one can teach the Dharma.

Once there was a village where no one had heard the Dharma. The men there were interested only in beautiful girls and nothing else. Avalokitesvara, the Bodhisattva of compassion, visited the village in the guise of a beautiful young woman carrying a fish basket. The men started pestering her, asking for fish, but really wanting her. She said, "I'm quite willing to marry the man who can memorize and recite the *Heart Sutra* in one day." All the men rushed home, and tried to memorize the sutra. The next day, after she heard all these recitations, she said, "Wonderful, but there are too many of you to choose from. I will marry whoever can memorize and recite the *Diamond Sutra* by tomorrow." The next day there were far fewer men, but still more than one. She said, "Still too many to choose from. Whoever memorizes the *Lotus Sutra,* that's the one I will marry."

The next day only one man returned, a very intelligent man. He had memorized all three sutras. Avalolkitesvara, as the woman, agreed to marry him, but after the wedding, that very same day, she became deathly ill. Before she died, she said to her husband, "I hope that after I die you will not forget the sutras."

Her husband replied, "I'll never forget you or the sutras." Then she died, but the next day she appeared before him. Frightened, he asked, "Who are you? Are you human or ghost?"

"Neither," she answered, "I am Avalokitesvara. I came to your village because the people had no faith in Buddhadharma. Now, with my help, you can start the villagers on the Buddha path."

Avalokitesvara incarnated as a beautiful woman to help people obsessed with lust. If the men had been obsessed with money, the Bodhisattva would have embodied a different incarnation and used a different approach.

On retreats I give people different methods. Some silently chant prayers, some use a *hua-t'ou,* others count breaths. Even with counting breaths, a seemingly simple method, there are many variations, and each variation suits a particular person.

A master should assess the student and then prescribe what he feels is the most useful method. The next student must be assessed anew. Indiscriminately handing out the same *kung-an* to everybody would prove to be fruitless. Of course, a *kung-an* used centuries ago may be used today, but only in situations where the master feels it will work.

A *kung-an* or teaching from the past can come alive under the right circumstances. But if a student cannot breathe life into a method, then no matter what it is or where it comes from, it is a dead method.

> *Rejecting words or clinging to them are both*
> *mistakes,*
> *Like a blazing fire, useful but dangerous.*

These lines may be viewed from two different levels: that of the practitioner and that of the already enlightened being. If you are a practitioner who deliberately seeks the precious mirror, then you will move further away rather than towards your goal. You should not cling to the idea of attaining enlightenment.

On the other hand, if you say, "I don't care about enlightenment. I don't care if it exists, or if I ever attain it," again you will never see the precious mirror in this lifetime. You cannot chase it, and you cannot run away from it.

What is the proper attitude? You should incorporate vows into your practice. Each time, before practicing, vow to work hard, vow to attain enlightenment. Yes, you should seek enlightenment, but when you sit, and use your method, all thoughts of seeking must vanish. There is nothing to seek; there is nothing to gain or lose. Just practice. Vows strengthen determination. Every sitting should begin with a sincere vow.

On another level, this couplet applies to a person who is already enlightened. Truly liberated beings are unaware of their power and wisdom. Their wisdom is ever-present, and they respond to every situation spontaneously.

The blazing fire in the poem represents the precious mirror. It is a beacon of wisdom, a source of power. Like fire, it can be beneficial, but it can also be dangerous. Cling to it and you will burn. Reject it and you will freeze. At one extreme are people who cannot accept the Dharma, and who will eventually reject the practice. At the other extreme are people who are obsessed with attaining enlightenment. They may fall into demonic states.

If a person has seen the precious mirror, and says, "I have the precious mirror!" then he cannot be fully liberated. It is a false enlightenment. He still clings to an "idea" of a precious mirror, to an idea of an "I" who is abiding in something.

I have seen people obsessed with enlightenment, and they have suffered because of it. Some of them believe they are enlightened, but they are not, and this causes many problems. Others get so disturbed about not reaching enlightenment that they become destructive, or even go insane. Truly, these people are burned by the fire. But an enlightened person becomes the fire, so he cannot be disturbed by it. He does not know that he is fire, but when someone needs the flame, he is there to bestow it. That fire is wisdom.

If it is only expressed in language
The precious mirror will be stained.

Any conception of enlightenment, even that of a precious mirror, is wrong. To have a conception is to stain the mirror, or to paint over it. No matter how beautiful a picture you paint, the mirror no longer reflects.

I have been to restaurants with mirror-covered walls, which give an illusion of spaciousness. But if someone were to write on a wall, "This is a mirror," then the illusion would be ruined. Left alone, the mirror reflects, but once something covers it, the reflection disappears.

There was a Ch'an master who was asked, "What is it like after enlightenment?"

He answered, "It can't be described. If you try to describe it, anything you say will be wrong."

The person who asked was pouring rice gruel from a large pot into small bowls. When he heard the answer, he said, "What a nice pot of gruel. Too bad it has been defiled by some rat shit."

Even saying that enlightenment is inconceivable or indescribable is wrong. Any description stains the precious mirror.

In the *Vimalakirti Sutra*, the Bodhisattva Vimalakirti did not answer such questions. That is the true answer. Even a gesture is better than words.

Although words such as "inconceivable" and "indescribable" do appear in the sutras, they are part of rational explanations that help convey the gradual teachings. Ch'an rarely uses these words because they are indirect. If the story I just told you involved an enlightened Ch'an master, a more reasonable answer to the question might have been, "Let's eat the gruel. There's no point in discussing this." That is direct.

If an enlightened Ch'an master answered such questions, it would be like painting a mirror or leaving rat shit in rice gruel. It is not important that students believe a master is enlightened, as long as they benefit from his teachings.

> *At midnight it is truly bright;*
> *By daylight it no longer shows.*

Common sense tells us that midnight is dark, daylight bright. But the poem does not speak of light; it speaks of the precious mirror, namely self-nature.

Self-nature does not change. The environment changes. The mirror does not darken in Samsara (delusion), and it does not brighten in enlightenment. In enlightenment self-nature does not manifest and become visible, and in Samsara self-nature is not defiled. You do not practice in order to make self-nature manifest. You practice to eliminate vexations. When vexations disappear, self-nature manifests naturally. It is not that self-nature appears; rather, vexation disappears. This is an important point to remember: Enlightenment is not the emergence of something new; it is the removal of vexation. Anything else would just be adding to your already deluded mind.

> *It serves as the law which governs all*
> *things;*
> *Use it to uproot all suffering.*

Previously, I emphasized that practice affects vexations, not self-nature, because self-nature is unchanging. So why talk about self-nature? You cannot change it or make it manifest. Of what use is the concept at all? The Buddha speaks about self-nature in order to help sentient beings who still need to practice. Self-nature is meaningless to the Buddha and the patriarchs, but they speak of an enlightened state so that they may urge ordinary beings to strive toward the precious mirror.

Sentient beings need goals and attachments, so it is necessary to speak of a precious mirror. That is why Tung-shan wrote the *Song of the Precious Mirror Samadhi*. The teachings speak of goals, of attachment, of an enlightened state, but when we practice, we must adopt an attitude of not seeking, not naming. In this way we progress. A target must be set, but it is a false target. People need it for incentive and direction, but it is only a device. If you practice correctly, the target disappears when you reach it. If the target is still there, then you have not reached it. The target is non-attachment. When there is no attachment, there is no suffering.

For instance, in the relationship between teacher and student, there should be no attachment to labels. The teacher should not think: "I am the teacher and he is the student." If such thoughts exist, problems will arise, because the teacher and student are attached to illusory concepts. With this kind of attitude, a teacher might get upset if the student were to rebel or leave.

The correct attitude should be: "If you treat me like a teacher, then I am a teacher; if you treat me as something else, then that is what I am."

In your everyday life, it would be upsetting if a friend left you, or an enemy troubled you, or a friend became an enemy. The Buddha speaks of the suffering that arises in people who are dear to one another and must separate, or in people who are hostile toward one another and must come into conflict.

> *Though it is not a way of action*
> *Still, it is not without words.*

"Way of action" is rendered from the two Sanskrit terms – *samskritta* and *asamskritta*. These terms can be interpreted as "dharmas with construction" and "dharmas without construction." General Buddhist philosophy states that any dharmas in the worldly realm of phenomena, both external and internal, are dharmas with construction, or dharmas of action, because they are constantly changing. According to this line of thought, dharmas with construction are separate and distinguishable from dharmas without construction, which is the unchanging state of self-nature.

Ch'an perspective, however, is different. Even though the precious mirror is not a dharma with construction, it is wrong to say that it is separate from it. Therefore, it is wrong to say that it is unnecessary to explain the precious mirror. Previously, the song said that speaking about enlightenment stains the precious mirror. Here, the song suggests more. In reality, the precious mirror is not stained by language. However, it is also not separate from language.

From the Sixth Patriarch onward, the emphasis in Ch'an has been that *bodhi* is the same as vexation. The same holds true for Nirvana and Samsara, for dharmas with construction (*samskritta*) and dharmas without construction (*asamskritta*).

> *As before the precious mirror,*
> *The form and reflection gaze on each other.*
> *You are not it,*
> *But it is just you.*

These lines allude to an event in Tung-shan Liang-chieh's life. He had been practicing many years but had not attained enlightenment. One day while crossing a river, he saw his reflection in the water. At that moment he understood his original nature. When he looked down into the water, he said, "I am Tung-shan and the reflection is Tung-shan, but really, which of the two is the true person?"

Ordinarily, one would say that the physical body is the real person and the reflection is the illusion, but Tung-shan felt that if the body is the true person, then the reflection is also the true person, because neither can exist without the other.

One might think that if there is no water, then there

can be no reflection, but this is not really the case. The reflection is always present; it is just that without water it simply cannot be seen. If you have a body, you have a reflection. If you have no reflection, you have no body.

Some schools of Buddhism state that the physical body is different and separate from the Dharma body. According to this view, the Dharma body is assumed when we free ourselves from the physical body. From the perspective of most Mahayana schools of Buddhism, if you believe you can transcend an "illusory" physical body to find a "true and undefiled" Dharma body, you will have more luck finding a rabbit with horns or a turtle with hair.

Tung-shan saw his original nature, his Dharma body. He saw that his physical body is not the Dharma body, but he also saw that the Dharma body is not separate from the physical body. The two bodies are not the same, yet they are not different. The physical body is nothing more than the physical body; it cannot encompass the Dharma body. But the Dharma body, which is not limited by space or time, is not separate from the physical body. The illusory body and mind are shadows or reflections of this undefiled Dharma body.

You cannot know a mirror exists until you see a reflection in it. You cannot see a reflection unless a mirror reflects it. The mirror and reflection are interdependent. They are not the same; they are not separate. If you truly understand this, then you understand the precious mirror.

There is another way to understand these verses. Earlier I said the physical body is a reflection in the precious mirror, or Dharma body. Now I say this: When you begin to practice, you begin with a physical body and mind – the precious mirror does not exist for you. When you see body and mind as reflections, you realize they are illusory, and you realize that the mirror's function is to reflect illusions. In reality, both *reflection* and *reflector* are illusory.

> *Just as an infant*
> *Is equipped with five sense organs.*

There is nothing intrinsically different between the Buddha and us. The only difference is that we have not realized our Buddha-nature. To give an analogy, we are to the Buddha as an infant is to an adult. In China, people who practice Buddhadharma are called, *fo-tze,* which literally translates as "Buddha's son." This is commonly interpreted to mean that we are disciples of Buddha. A second interpretation holds that we are the sons of the Buddha, and in fact, the eldest sons of the Buddha. One day we too will inherit, or attain, Buddhahood.

An infant is not an adult, but it has the potential to be one. Still, an infant needs adults to care for it, to nurture and teach it. In the same way, practitioners of Buddhadharma need the Buddhas, Bodhisattvas, the Three Jewels, masters and teachers to care for them and guide them. Infants reach adulthood; so also will practitioners reach Buddhahood.

The five sense organs of the infant referred to in the poem can be taken to mean the Buddha's five Dharma bodies, which are derived from the five merits of the Buddha: precepts, samadhi, wisdom, liberation, and the wisdom derived from liberation. The first wisdom, also known as root wisdom, is the wisdom which manifests when self-nature is revealed – when vexations disappear. The wisdom derived from liberation is ultimate wisdom, or acquired wisdom, and so is specified as a separate Dharma body, a separate merit. Acquired wisdom is used to help other sentient beings.

The essence of these five merits is within everyone. If we take the Five Precepts (no killing, no stealing, no sexual misconduct, no lying, no intoxicants), then we are in accordance, at least partially, with the "precept" Dharma body of the Buddha. With respect to wisdom, even an intellectual understanding of the sutras brings us into partial accordance with the "wisdom" Dharma body. Even if we do not attain ultimate liberation, but only relative liberation, we still come into accordance with the "wisdom derived from liberation" Dharma body. We have the seeds of these merits, these Dharma bodies, but since we are infants, we need to develop them.

> *It neither comes nor goes,*
> *It neither arises nor abides.*

These lines clarify certain misconceptions about Samsara and Nirvana. You may think that in attaining Buddhahood you leave Samsara and enter Nirvana. You may think that Buddhas and Bodhisattvas travel from Nirvana to Samsara to help sentient beings. Such is the understanding of many Buddhists. But these concepts only serve as convenient explanations, expedient teachings. They are not ultimate teachings.

Samsara and Nirvana are not things, nor are they places. These verses describe Buddhahood. The Buddha is a perfect being, not limited by restrictions of space and time. Many Buddhists may think that transcending Samsara involves space. They believe that the Buddha, who has transcended the three realms, must be somewhere else, and that he must return to help sentient beings. But Buddha is not separate from us. The term *Tathagata*, sometimes called True Suchness, has the meaning: "thus go/thus come." This is a better understanding. "Transcending the three realms," "returning to Samsara to help sentient beings" – these are expedient teachings, not ultimate teachings.

Many Buddhists speak of people with virtuous karmic seeds, who, with the proper causes and conditions, bloom into a serious practitioners. Such people, they believe, reach a point in their practice where their faith is firmly established and attainment and will not regress. This is just another expedient teaching. The True Suchness of each sentient being is the same as that of the Buddha. The karmic seed is this True Suchness. There is no sprouting, no progression, no regression.

In reality, the precious mirror is not within us. It cannot be found in Buddhadharma, in the Ch'an hall, or through our practice. If self-nature can be discovered only through the teachings or through a particular practice, then that state cannot be genuine. If you say that the mirror is already within you, that you are already the Buddha, that is not the proper attitude.

The proper attitude is this: "I need to practice to attain the precious mirror, although the precious mirror is not something that I attain through practice." This may sound strange, but it is correct. Perhaps it is best to leave it at that, and just practice.

> P'o-p'o H'o-h'o –
> A phrase without meaning.
> You can never get the substance of it
> Because the language is not correct.

Human beings use sounds to communicate. When someone talks, there is always meaning in what is said, even if the meaning is nonsense. But, I have a question: When people talk, do they really say anything?

I saw a woman who had been talking to another woman for a long time. I asked her, "Is she a friend of yours?"

She said, "Not really. We just met."

So I asked, "What is there to talk about, then?"

"Nothing really," she admitted, "but it's a good way to pass the time. Besides, after talking, we became friends."

I also read that there is a telephone service for people who want to talk but have no one to talk with. They can dial a number and listen to conversations and add their own comments, if they are interested.

These examples show that ordinary people need to

communicate. Without conversation, they would suffer, so talk makes them feel better. But are they really saying anything when they talk? Probably not.

Is talk about the precious mirror any more fruitful than these conversations I have mentioned? Probably not. The phrase "P'o-p'o H'o-h'o" has absolutely no meaning. Likewise all the illustrations and explanations we use to describe the precious mirror really have no meaning and cannot tell us what the precious mirror truly is. Nonetheless, we continue with our explanations, because people need them.

No matter how you try to explain the precious mirror, no matter which language or symbols you choose, you cannot come close to the meaning. Try it with something more familiar. In ancient China, a description of a beautiful woman involved analogies: her eyes like a phoenix, her face the shape of a watermelon seed, her teeth like white seashells, her mouth shaped like a cherry, her fingers like scallions. Think about these images – they are really not too flattering. Even something so familiar as a human being is difficult to describe with words. Imagine, then, how difficult it is to describe the precious mirror.

Masters and patriarchs are much like babies, making nonsense sounds trying to speak. They know what they have experienced, they know what they want to say, but there is no way they can say it.

We now come to the core of the poem, so I will take care in explaining these difficult lines:

> Doubling the Li trigram makes six lines.
> The outer and inner lines mutually interact.
> Stacked, they become three pairs;
> At most they can transform into five.

In this stanza, Tung-shan borrows symbols from the *I Ching* to illustrate the central ideas of the Ts'ao-tung sect. Ts'ao-tung masters speak of five levels of attainment by which they gauge practitioners' progress. Although the philosophy of the *I Ching* differs from that of Buddhism, some ideas and imagery serve as useful tools to help explain Ts'ao-tung concepts.

The *I Ching* uses solid and broken lines in combinations of three (i.e., trigrams) to explain the interaction of active (yang) and passive (yin) forces. A solid line represents yang, a broken line represents yin. In illustrating the path of spiritual attainment, Tung-shan uses these lines to represent opposites, or extremes, such as Samsara and Nirvana, vexation and wisdom.

The phrase, "outer and inner" of the second line can also be understood as "off-center and center." Like yin and yang, off-center and center represent absolutes. Buddhism speaks of absolutes, such as True Suchness and Samsara. But really, there is no such thing as an absolute. There is always interaction between extremes. If True Suchness existed alone, there would be no way to experience it. You would have nothing to compare it to.

Where there is one, there must be two. There can be none, but never only one. True Suchness exists only in relation to Samsara, just as wisdom exists only in relation to vexation.

In this poem, the inner and outer, or center and off-center, refer to vexation and wisdom. You might think that wisdom should be the center and vexation the off-center, but the ideas are drawn from a fundamental principle of the Ch'an sect, which states that *bodhi* (wisdom) is vexation and vexation is *bodhi.* Vexation and wisdom interact in different ways, depending on the level of attainment of the practitioner. I will use a circle as a visual symbol to help explain what is meant by center and off-center. Five circles, with varying degrees of white and black shading, represent the five levels of attainment described by Ts'ao-tung sect. The first, and shallowest, of the five levels does not correspond to beginning practitioners, but rather, to those who have already seen their original nature.

The first level is called "The off-center within the center." The off-center is wisdom, the center is vexation. Here, the practitioner, still immersed in vexation (black), has revealed the precious mirror (white). He has begun to experience wisdom. For the first time, the practitioner sees his original nature, and he now has the faith to continue practicing diligently. Though he still abides in vexation, the practitioner is completely focused on experiencing wisdom.

The second level is called "The center within the off-center." In this circle, the white of wisdom dominates the black of vexation. But although more and more wisdom has been revealed, the practitioner is now keenly aware of and totally focused on his remaining vexation. He is in the process of eliminating vexation.

The third level is literally translated as "coming in the center," but it is better understood as "manifesting in the midst of essence." Here, vexations no longer manifest externally, but the practitioner realizes that they still exist. It is better to view this circle three dimensionally, as a sphere, with the dark core of vexation completely covered by the white shell of wisdom. Vexations are tame; they manifest only in the center. Potentially, they can still arise. At this level, for the first time, the practitioner is equally aware of both vexation and wisdom. It is known as the pivot of the five levels.

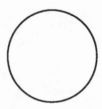

The fourth level is loosely translated as "arrival with dual aspects." The dual aspects are the center and off-center – vexation and wisdom. The title of the third circle – "coming in the center" – implies movement in a particular direction. At the fourth level, the practitioner has arrived at his destination. The circle is completely white. It would seem, according to our use of black and white, that wisdom has completely eradicted vexation. But it is not the case. As I said earlier, there can be two, but never one. With the removal of vexation, wisdom also disappears. Really, to best represent this stage, we should draw nothing – just leave a blank space. The outline of a circle is drawn for purposes of illustration.

Wisdom disappears because it can manifest only in the world of Samsara, in the realm of phenomena. When there is total stillness, there can be no wisdom. The wisdom of the fourth level is known as fundamental, or root, wisdom.

This is true liberation, complete emptiness. Samsara is transcended, the cycle of birth and death is broken. The fourth level is the stage of no-action, of nothingness. There are no sentient beings, so there is nothing to be saved.

The fifth circle is called "perfection on both counts." The fourth level is "fundamental wisdom." The fifth level is "acquired wisdom." The fourth level is total emptiness; nothing exists. At the fifth level, vexation *is* wisdom. That is why the circle is completely black. A being at the fifth level again relates to the world of phenomena, but he uses vexation as a tool of wisdom to help sentient beings.

Ordinary sentient beings think that such a person still suffers from vexation. But to someone at the fifth level, this very vexation is wisdom. At this level, he fully participates in the world and helps sentient beings.

Double Li Trigram

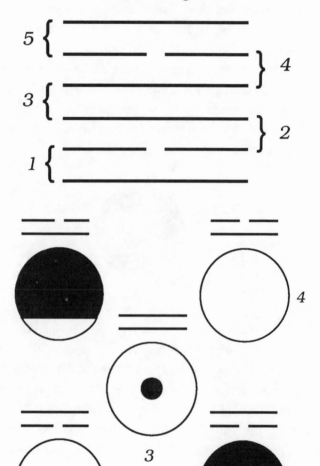

In the preceding paragraphs, circles have been used to illustrate the five levels of attainment. Tung-shan uses the doubled Li trigram for the same purpose – to illustrate the five levels of attainment. He says that the three pairs transform into five. If you look at the hexigram in the diagram above, you see that the six lines can be separated into five pairs. However, two sets of pairs, pairs 1 and 4, and 2 and 5, are the same. In fact, there are only three pairs, yet they transform into the five levels I just spoke about.

In the preceding diagram, each circle is matched with a set of paired lines. To understand Tung-shan's symbols, realize that the solid line corresponds to the white part of the circle and represents wisdom. The broken line correponds to black and represents vexation. Pairs 1 and 2 should really be taken together. They represent the practitioner's beginning realization of wisdom and progressive removal of vexation. Pair 3, as I mentioned before, is the pivot, where the practitioner is equally aware of both wisdom and vexation. Pairs 4 and 5 should also be taken together; they represent the final stages of enlightenment.

To briefly summarize: at level one the practitioner is focused on wisdom, whereas at level two he is focused on vexation. The point, however, is that the emphasis is still on practice.

At the fourth and fifth levels, practice is no longer an issue. The emphasis is on wisdom derived from liberation and helping sentient beings. At the fourth level, ultimate liberation, neither wisdom nor vexation exist.

There are no sentient beings to be saved. At the fifth level, vexation is wisdom, and it can be used to help sentient beings.

At level three, practice is still necessary. The practitioner is still part of the world of Samsara, yet at a stage where he can help sentient beings, where vexations no longer manifest.

> Like the five aromas of the hyssop plant
> Or the five branches of the vajra sceptre.
> The exact center subtly harmonizing,
> Drumming and singing simultaneously.

The first two lines continue to explain the five levels of attainment of the Ts'ao-tung sect. The hyssop plant has five subtle aromas or flavors. It is said that if you taste one flavor, then in fact you have had a taste of all of them. One flavor suggests the other four flavors. Likewise, there are five branches, or arcs, on the head of a *vajra* sceptre, but if you hold onto one arc, the others will follow.

How does this relate to the five levels of attainment? Since the outer and inner – wisdom and vexation – mutually interact, attaining any of the five levels places a practitioner in a position to attain the others; each level contains the other four, because they are all involved, in one way or another, with wisdom and vexation.

These levels do not really exist, but such distinctions are made to help sentient beings in their practice. If there were one level, separate from everything else, then it would not be attainable, because nothing would be connected to it. Since we are all innately Buddhas, the potential to attain these five levels is always within us.

The next two lines refer to the third level, the pivot. As I said earlier, it is at the third level that a person is equally aware of vexation and wisdom. He is different from a person at the fifth level, who knows vexation and wisdom are the same. The third level connects enlightened beings at the fourth and fifth levels (those who have fully realized wisdom and who help sentient beings) with ordinary sentient beings at the first and second levels (those who are concerned with eliminating vexation).

Drumming and singing refer to the third level, where all the wonderful and subtle functions of the five levels become manifest. The subtle, wonderful functions eliminate vexations and are used to help others. At this level, however, there is still a need for practice, and if the person is truly determined, he will look for the help of a great master.

The preceding eight lines of verse are the core of the *Song of the Precious Mirror Samadhi.* The five levels of attainment, known collectively as the "Five Levels of Lord and Vassal," are used by the Ts'ao-tung sect, and Tung-shan was the first master to speak of the five levels in this way (where vexation is the center and wisdom is the off-center). Other Ts'ao-tung masters used different variations. Similarly, the Lin-chi sect uses the four positions of "host and guest" to describe a person's level of practice and experience of wisdom and vexation. You might ask why Ch'an speaks of "sudden enlightenment" and at the same time talks about levels of enlightenment and stages of practice. You must understand that these schemes and descriptions are used by teachers to evaluate their students' attainment, and to help them along the path toward ultimate enlightenment.

Centuries later, during the Ming and Ching dynasties, masters spoke of the "Three Barriers" of practice. These barriers correspond to the first three levels of the Ts'ao-tung sect's five categories. The first barrier is seeing into one's nature. The second barrier, known as the multiple barrier, describes the stage where the person continues to practice, deepening his awareness of self-nature and eliminating vexations. The third barrier is called the prison barrier. Breaking through this barrier, a practitioner breaks out of the prison of Samsara. Once a person breaks through the third barrier, or passes the third level, progress through the fourth level to the fifth level is quite natural.

> *Penetrate the goal and you will fathom the way.*
> *In order to lead there must be a road.*
> *To be wrong is auspicious;*
> *Do not oppose it.*

The goal is the precious mirror – the mind completely free of any obstruction or impurity. The path refers to all the methods, understanding and reasoning that people use to attain the Buddha Mind.

A Chinese character in the third line of this stanza has two meanings. The first meaning, "to be wrong," is used in this translation. Earlier, in describing the five levels of attainment, I drew a darkened circle, where black meant vexation, and said that this is the highest level. So that which is wrong is, in fact, most right. Vexation, which is most wrong, is just this highest wisdom.

The character's second meaning is "interaction between two things." The unfolding of wisdom and vexation throughout the five levels of attainment is auspicious. In traveling the path to enlightenment, one must move through these levels of interaction, and not resist them. It is the movement through these five levels that brings the practitioner true understanding of the practice.

> Natural and subtle
> It is neither ignorance nor enlightenment.
> Causes and conditions have their time and
>   season,
> Tranquil and illuminating.

At this point, the song returns to the precious mirror. It is both natural and subtle. "Natural" refers to an undefiled, unmoving state. "Subtle" refers to the illuminating power of the mirror – its power to function. Both of these attributes are necessary. Do not mistake a state of naturalness alone for the precious mirror.

There was an ancient Indian tradition which believed in pure nature – that the world is nothing more than what can be seen, heard, felt, tasted, and smelled. Believing only in pure nature, they had no concern for society, spiritual progress, or suffering. They had no particular interest in explaining why things are the way they are. They did not believe that actions of the past determine the present and actions of the present determine the future. In such a system of beliefs, human life has no meaning.

The power of the mirror to illuminate, in conjunction with the attribute of naturalness, makes the wondrous mirror complete. "Natural" is the unchanging state of Buddha-nature. "Subtle" is Buddha-nature manifesting as wisdom.

When he realized Buddhahood, Sakyamuni said, "It is wonderful – all sentient beings have the inherent wisdom and merit of the Buddha." *Bodhi* is ever-present. It need not be attained, only realized. Vexations are illusory, and constantly change, but *bodhi* is unchanging. Merit and wisdom are not derived from the practice. They are uncovered by the practice.

Some say that there is a seed of *bodhi*, and with practice this seed will sprout and ripen, but this is incorrect. The *bodhi* seed does not ripen, for if it did, it would also have to decay.

Natural and subtle, the precious mirror is neither enlightenment nor ignorance. Whether you are enlightened or ignorant, the precious mirror is there. When you are enlightened, *bodhi* manifests. When you are in Samsara, *bodhi* is covered by vexation.

There is a story about a prince in rags who roamed throughout his kingdom. People thought he was a beggar, and they treated him like one. When his retainers realized who he really was, they brought him into the palace. We are like that prince, but in our ignorance we forget, and we act more like beggars. The story never tells us when the prince became a beggar. Similarly, since beginningless time, we have wandered aimlessly in a state of ignorance.

> *It is so small it enters the spaceless,*
> *So large it is beyond dimension.*

These lines also speak about the precious mirror. The enlightened mind does not move, yet it functions. It is not dead; rather, it is inconceivably more powerful than the mind of vexation, which, because of its attachments, is limited to a small realm of thought and experience. The enlightened mind has no attachments, and so has unlimited power. It can function in realms too small to measure, and on scales larger than space itself. Ordinarily, our knowledge and experience are limited. We cannot comprehend absolute Buddha-nature, which exists everywhere. The enlightened mind has no such limitations; it has realized the true nature of reality. This is not the result of scientific investigation or intellectual endeavor. It is direct personal experience.

> *If you are off by a hair's breadth*
> *Then you would be out of harmony.*

In the Chinese version of this poem, there is a word that corresponds to a musical instrument. If it is tuned a hair too tight or loose, the sound will be out of tune. If it is tuned perfectly, the tone is beautiful. Likewise, if the precious mirror is even the slightest bit stained, then it no longer manifests as the true wonderful mirror.

Although other religions and certain individuals speak of enlightenment experiences, there is an important difference between their descriptions and that of Mahayana Buddhism. In genuine Mahayana Buddhist enlightenment there are no attachments. Therefore, a practitioner must pass through different levels, continually eliminating attachments, before this final stage of enlightenment is reached.

After a deep experience, it is difficult for a practitioner to determine whether vexations are still present. A good teacher must verify the level of attainment. He might use the five levels described in this poem to measure the practitioner's attainment. If attachment is present, the experience is not genuine Ch'an.

> Now there is sudden and gradual
>   (enlightenment)
> In order to establish the fundamental guidelines.
> When the fundamental guidelines are clear
> They become the rule.
> Realization of the basic principle is the
>   ultimate standard,
> Genuine, constant, yet flowing,

We really cannot talk about Ch'an. But to understand, we are forced to speak. Enlightenment is always sudden, but one may practice vigorously or gently.

Since Ch'an enlightenment is sudden, there is really no need to discuss the stages of a practitioner's practice. Yet we do so in order to determine whether a practitioner has indeed become enlightened, and if he has, how thorough his enlightenment is. It is for this reason that the Ts'ao-tung sect speaks of five levels of attainment.

Only when enlightenment is genuine will the precious mirror truly manifest in a constant manner. Until this happens, the enlightened mind will gradually disappear under a cloud of vexation and move into delusion again.

> With still body but racing mind,
> Like a tethered horse or a mouse frozen by
>   fright.
> Past sages pitied them
> And liberated them with Buddhadharma.
> Following their upside down ways
> They took black for white.
> When inverted thinking disappears,
> They realize Mind of their own accord.

These eight lines describe people who have experienced false enlightenment. Although they seem to be enlightened and free of vexation, their vexations are only tamed and suppressed. The fundamental problems have not been resolved, and therefore the enlightenment is not genuine.

These eight lines especially address people who practice *samadhi*. Ch'an is not opposed to *samadhi*, but it is opposed to attachment to the *samadhi* experience. *Samadhi* is better than any other wordly experience. There is tremendous risk of becoming attached to it; some people would rather die than come out of it.

Samadhi produces a calm mind, a stable mind. Some wisdom may manifest. It enhances strong faith in the practice. But it is not Ch'an. The tethered horse and frozen mouse refer to such a mind. The mind is contained, vexations are tamed. Nonetheless, the potential for vexations to arise is still there, and therefore, the problem has not been resolved.

An active volcano may look beautiful and serene, but at any moment it can erupt. So, too, a person in *samadhi* suppresses but does not eradicate vexations. When *samadhi* power subsides, vexations will reemerge. Such practitioners are followers of the upside-down ways, who take black for white. *Samadhi* is a temporary, wordly experience. People who believe that it is ultimate enlightenment lack a fundamental understanding of Buddhadharma.

People who experience shallow *samadhi* will soon confront vexations again, and so come to realize that they are not enlightened. But people who have experienced deep states of *samadhi* may feel they have completely eradicated vexations. However, they are still attached to *samadhi* itself. The last two lines in this section state that if such people can accept the principles of Buddhadharma and correct their attitude, then in a short time they can become enlightened.

> *If you want to merge with the ancient track*
> *Then contemplate the ancients.*
> *At the completion of the Buddha Path*
> *Ten kalpas of contemplation will be*
> *   established.*

The ancient track is the path traveled by the ancient Buddhas. If we want to attain Buddhahood, then we must traverse this path. Some may feel that their personal path is just as good as the Buddha path, but this is not true. People speak of enlightened saints from the East, enlightened saints from the West. We should realize that there are different criteria for sainthood, but if a person is not on the ancient path of the Buddhas, then he is not a saint of the Buddhadharma.

We know of the Buddha path from the sutras – Sakyamuni describes it. It is the path he has illuminated for us. Although the Ch'an sect avoids language, symbols, or descriptions, it cautions us not to stray from the sutras' teachings by as much as a single word. To do so would be the same as accepting the teachings of demons.

A Ch'an practitioner can use the ancient track to clarify his experience, but it is posssible he may use his own knowledge and misinterpret the sutras, especialy if his experience is not genuine. This is dangerous. Therefore, it is important to have a teacher to confirm one's experience, to measure one's attainment, and to correct one's mistakes. One must not stray from the sutras when practicing Buddhadharma.

The "ten *kalpas*" in the song has at least two interpretations. The first interpretation is derived from the T'ien-tai school. This school has four teachings associated with it: Hinayana, Mahayana that is similar to Hinayana, Mahayana that is different from Hinayana, and the perfect teaching. It is the perfect teaching that speaks of ten levels of faith on the path to Buddhahood. The ten *kalpas* in the poem refer to the time needed to attain the tenth level of faith, which is that of the Buddha.

A second interpretation refers to a Bodhisattva mentioned in the sutras, who practiced for ten *kalpas*, but did not attain enlightenment. This is because he had no sutras to guide him. Without the guidance of the sutras, the practice of Buddhadharma is extremely difficult.

> *Like a tiger's lame foot,*
> *Like a shoeless horse,*

These two lines refer to a practitioner who neglects the sutras in his quest for Buddhahood. A lame tiger cannot hunt and is at the mercy of other animals. A shoeless horse cannot run far and is of no use in battle. Similarly, without the guidance of the sutras to teach, test and affirm attainment, a practitioner is in peril.

> *Because there is a defect*
> *You seek the jewelled bench and priceless*
>   *halter*

Because you are astonished
You realize you were like the brown or
white ox.

These verses describe the person who is a diligent practitioner but who has not yet uncovered his precious mirror. He wears the Buddha's teachings like adornments to impress other people with his intellectual knowledge and defective practice.

However, when he genuinely experiences for the first time that the precious mirror is already within him, he is astonished; and he realizes that before his experience he was no better than a dull and stupid ox.

Hou-i used his skill
To hit the target at a hundred paces.
As soon as the arrow hits the mark
Of what further use is his skill?

Hou-i is a legendary figure in China: a great archer who could pierce a leaf at a distance of a hundred meters. If we were as skilled in practice as Hou-i was in archery, we would make great and swift progress. Our skill is honed by the teachings of the sutras.

But after we see our self-nature and experience ultimate enlightenment, the skills and sutras are no longer necessary. They have served their purpose.

When a wooden man breaks into song,
A stone woman gets up to dance.

Since this cannot be understood by
  reasoning
How can it be analyzed?

A wooden man singing and a stone woman dancing? Ridiculous by ordinary peoples' standards, but quite reasonable in Ch'an – where there is no difference between sentience and non-sentience. Sentience and non-sentience are Buddha seeds from the same source. The non-sentient can speak the Dharma and reach Buddhahood, but this can only be understood by an enlightened being.

Ordinary people might use their reasoning or imagination to grasp this, but it would be of no use. An enlightened being, however, sees no difference between sentience and non-sentience. A wooden man might very well sing, but it would be a soundless song, and a stone woman might dance, but it would be a dance with no movement.

The minister serves his lord;
The son obeys his father.
If he does not obey, he is not filial;
If the minister does not serve, he is not loyal.

In these lines, the lord and father refer to the state of purity – the Buddha state, and the minister and son refer to the state of ordinary people. You must move toward the undefiled state by heeding the sutras. If you follow your own path, or misinterpret the sutras, you will fall into outer-path teachings. If you follow such a path, you are not a true Ch'an practitioner.

> *To cultivate in hiding, functioning in secret,*
> *Like a fool, like a dolt;*
> *If only you are able to persist,*
> *You will be called a master among masters.*

These are the last four lines of the poem. A great practitioner does not call attention to his practice. He practices quietly toward Buddhahood. Most people would regard him as an ordinary being, not a saint. Nonetheless, such a person possesses great wisdom and compassion. He helps sentient beings, and he derives great benefit from his practice. People might be blind to his wisdom and compassion, however, and call him a dolt or fool. It does not matter.

If you persist in your practice, and quietly cultivate Buddhadharma, eventually you will pass the most difficult barriers and reach the fifth level, where vexation and *bodhi* are the same. You will be a master among masters.